Overland

Overland

Peter Fraenkel

DAVID & CHARLES
NEWTON ABBOT   LONDON
NORTH POMFRET (VT)   VANCOUVER

ISBN 0 7153 7040 5 X

Library of Congress Catalog Card Number 75-26358

© Peter Fraenkel 1975

All rights reserved. No part of this publication may be reproduced, stored in a retrieval system, or transmitted, in any form or by any means, electronic, mechanical, photocopying, recording or otherwise, without the prior permission of David & Charles (Holdings) Limited

London Borough
of Enfield
Public Libraries

P25283

Set in 11 on 13pt Monotype Baskerville
and printed in Great Britain
by Latimer Trend & Company Ltd Plymouth
for David & Charles (Holdings) Limited
South Devon House Newton Abbot Devon

Published in United States of America
by David & Charles Inc
North Pomfret Vermont 05053 USA

Published in Canada
by Douglas David & Charles Limited
132 Philip Avenue North Vancouver BC

Contents

	page
Preface	7

Planning   11
   The Journey: Where, When, How · How Much Will It Cost? · Finding and Choosing Companions · Methods of Travel · Choosing a Vehicle

Preparation   31
   Paying For Your Trip · Carrying Money · Keeping Track of Costs · Personal Documents · Vehicle Documents · Vaccinations · Insurance · Mail

Equipment   47
   A Roof Over Your Head · Cooking Equipment · Personal Gear · Food, Stores and General Equipment · First Aid and Medical Equipment · Mechanic's Department: Tools and Spares · Vehicle Accessories and Modifications · Getting the Vehicle Ready · Packing and Loading

On the Road   76
   Drivers and Driving · Roads and Tracks · Navigation · Maintenance and Repairs

	page
Some Problems	108

    People Problems · Camping · Eating · Water · Haggling · Emergencies

Recording the Journey	132

    Keeping a Diary · Photography · Tape Recorders

Checklists: Equipment and Information	139
Appendix 1 personal and communal equipment	139
2 vehicle documents and equipment, etc.	141
3 medical kit	145
4 addresses	147
5 basic vocabularies	148
Bibliography	150
Index	153

Preface

In these days of high fuel prices and potential shortage, overlanders may wonder how much longer any but the wealthy will be able to afford long-distance travel, but in fact the cost of fuel is a relatively small proportion of the total cost of a journey. It may be that in the years ahead the conventional motor vehicle will be replaced by a form of transport yet to be developed, or that the overlander will return to travel on foot, camel, or donkey. Whatever happens, if you want to escape and head for new horizons the present is as good a time as any.

No book will provide all the answers to all the questions, but this one gives a broad idea of the conditions to be faced and should enable would-be travellers to plan an adequately equipped and documented trip.

Borders open, close and alter, costs increase and the overland scene itself is fluid; a book offering guidance is likely to be more valuable than one which attempts to lay down a set of rules, and it is more satisfactory—and certainly more prudent—to check a source for current information than to work on facts and figures which may be out of date within months of publication.

The author will be grateful to receive readers' suggestions, corrections and criticisms.

P.F.

All photographs in this book are from the author's photographic library.

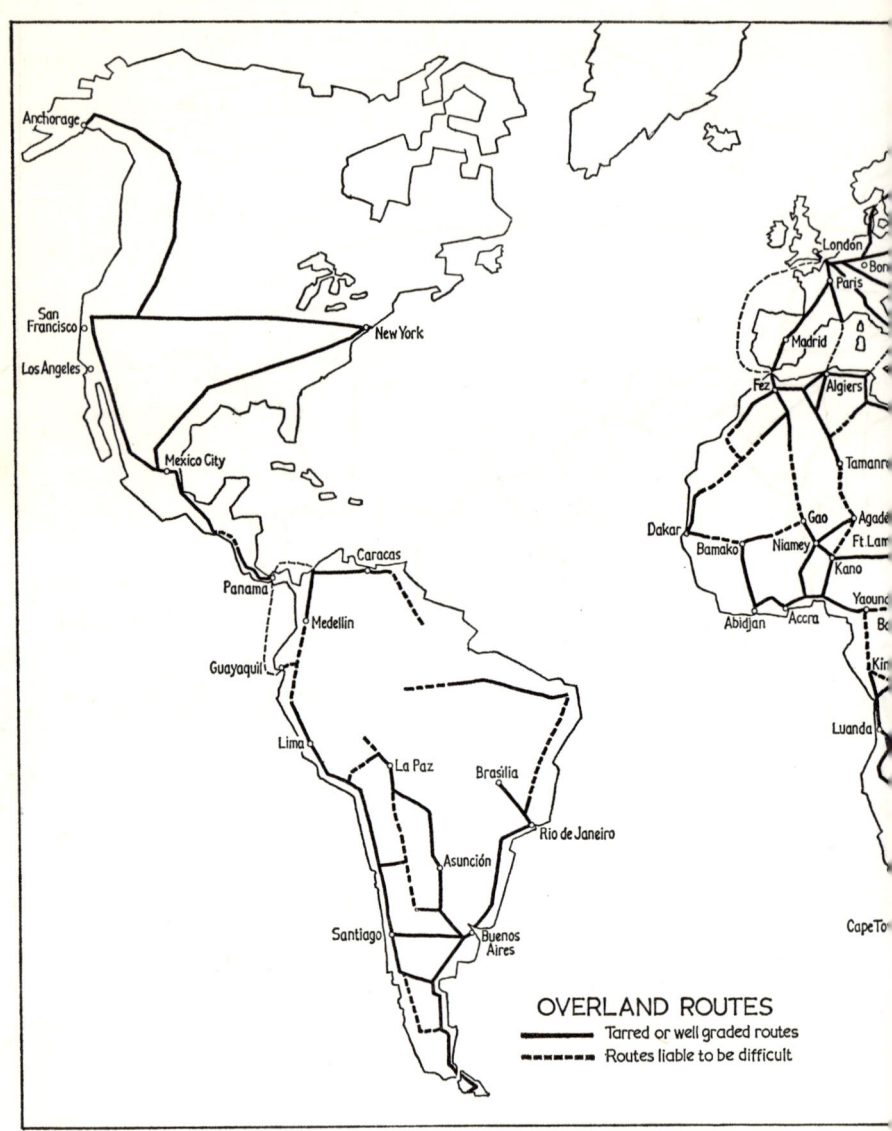

Note: while all routes shown are physically possib

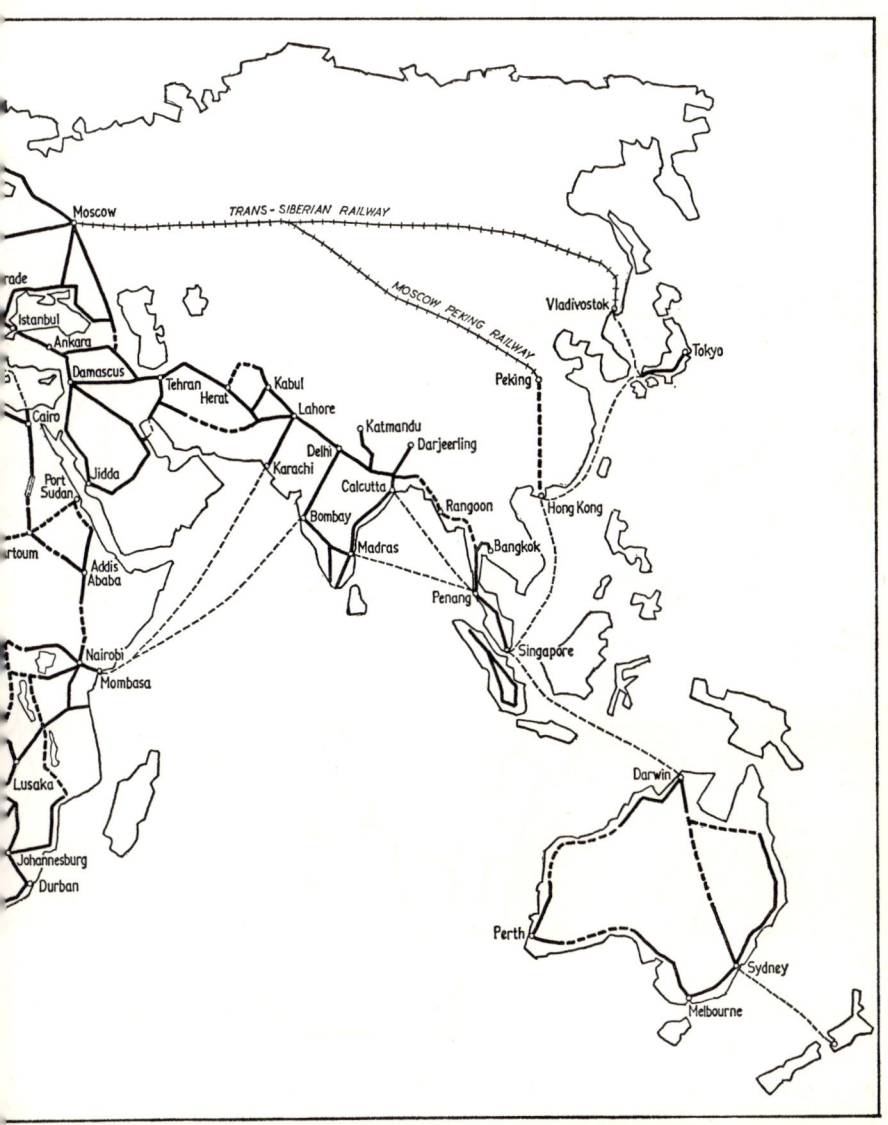

ne are temporarily closed for political reasons.

Planning

THE JOURNEY: WHERE, WHEN, HOW

Route restrictions
Many routes are impossible for political reasons. Some frontiers are permanently closed while others close from time to time; the situation is constantly changing. Natural obstacles to overland travel are more permanent and predictable, and deserts, jungles and mountains usually have tracks suitable for rugged vehicles. Difficulties are likely to be caused by extreme climatic conditions, and a check of rainfall and temperature at the proposed time of travel is essential.

Which continent?
For the majority of overlanders the choice will have to be between Africa and Asia, and this book consequently stresses these continents although the guidelines are applicable anywhere—in some details even to the 'hard' camper in remote parts of the UK. Europe offers interesting short routes and travellers to northern Scandinavia are able to get the taste of overland during a holiday of normal duration. The Americas offer plenty of scope—particularly the Pan American highway from Alaska through Central America to South America—but because of the cost of shipping a vehicle only a wealthy or sponsored minority can consider it if the starting place is Europe. Australia is similarly interesting but limited for the same reasons. The not-to-be-deterred traveller in the Americas

or Australia could investigate the possibility of getting there first, then buying and equipping a vehicle.

Fuel prices are generally much lower in Asia than in Africa and nearly all other costs are proportionately less, so a trans-African journey will cost nearly twice as much for a given distance. The political and physical problems will also be greater; not only will you need more visas, but the first major obstacle, the Sahara, should not be tackled in an ill-equipped or unsuitable vehicle.

The easiest and least expensive overland trip at present is via Istanbul to the east. This will provide a basic apprenticeship, and Africa can be tackled later. If you are really set on Africa it is important to cost your proposed trip realistically, allowing adequate reserves of money, for vehicle repairs in remote parts of Africa can be expensive. A less expensive taste of desert conditions can be obtained on a trip to southern Morocco, northern Algeria or Tunisia. Long before your wheel tracks in the sand have faded you will be planning a trans-Saharan expedition.

Sources of information

Once you have decided on a route, researching the details can be cheap in all except time. Some of the best sources of information are free brochures and maps issued by the embassies and tourist offices of the countries you hope to visit. Most countries with an established tourist trade maintain tourist offices in London, Paris, New York and similar centres, and even the smallest nations issue duplicated information sheets.

Tourist office maps are often the most reliable sources of information on the state of roads; the Turkish and the Iranian State Tourist organisations produce particularly good free maps, and the major oil companies sell useful road maps of countries where they market their products. Shell maps of Europe cover the territory as far as eastern Europe or North Africa. Trans-African travellers have no map problems as the Michelin 1 in 4,000,000 series (63 miles to the inch) covers the whole continent in three sheets. This series is outstandingly good as it sets out a wealth of useful detail on road conditions, distances, climatic conditions and places of interest. Larger-scale Michelin maps of Morocco and Ivory Coast are available, as is a complete coverage of western Europe, but the series does not extend to Asia. Commercially published maps, available from bookshops, rarely give details of road conditions.

Stanfords of London specialise in maps and guide books, and can often supply government-produced survey maps of little-known parts of the world and large-scale physical maps of areas you may wish to investigate in detail.

The best sources of information on what to see along the route are books by other travellers; if reading time is short, picture books, usually available from libraries, will provide an impression of what there is to see. A little-known but extremely valuable source of information is the travel notes produced from time to time by British embassies, high commissions and consulates in almost all the countries where Great Britain has diplomatic representation. The content varies, but most give details of climate, currency, regulations, customs, border crossings, language and sometimes places of interest. The notes are generally available from the Consular Department of the Foreign and Commonwealth Office, London. This service is intended to help British travellers, but nationals of other countries will usually find that their own foreign service produces similar notes.

Two further major sources of useful information are the Automobile Association and the Royal Automobile Club. If one of your party is already a member, routes and other information will be available free and a number of useful handbooks at reduced prices. These organisations have a monopoly in issuing such essential vehicle documents as the carnet de passage, and membership is necessary. AA and RAC information on Europe is generally reliable, but less so for places further afield.

Weather conditions

The best time to leave Europe for Africa or Asia is September or October, too early for severe winter conditions in Europe and the highlands of Turkey and Iran, but enabling the Sahara or India to be reached during the cool months of November or December. India is extremely hot from April until the monsoon breaks in June, when travel is difficult until the rains end in October. The Sahara is particularly inhospitable between April and October because of intense summer heat and violent sandstorms that can blow for days. Turkey and the higher parts of Iran and Afghanistan can be visited at almost any time of the year except from December to February, when temperatures on the mountain passes drop low enough to freeze diesel fuel. These regions are at their best during the brief spring in April and May, but are also comfortable in September and October.

HOW MUCH WILL IT COST?

The three basic cost elements are pre-departure costs, costs related to distance, and costs related to total travelling time.

Pre-departure costs

These include buying, preparing and overhauling a suitable vehicle, plus the cost of all necessary equipment, spares and stores. Allowance can be made for income from selling the vehicle and other equipment.

Additional costs will be those for vehicle documents and insurance, cross-Channel ferry fares if you are travelling from Britain, and personal documents such as passports, driving licences and visas. There will also be expenditure on maps, correspondence, telephone calls and errand-running.

Most individuals will have to budget for extra clothes, perhaps a sleeping bag and other camping gear, sunglasses and a supply of film.

Costs related to distance

The costs of running your vehicle will be roughly proportional to the distance covered. They will include expenditure on fuel, repairs, servicing, compulsory insurance bought at borders, road tolls and further ferry fares.

Fuel prices vary greatly from country to country, and considerable economies can be made by buying fuel where it is cheapest, and it may sometimes be cheaper to choose a longer route through countries with low fuel prices. Divide your route into fuel price zones when working out running costs and remember that you can often travel a couple of hundred miles into an expensive zone on petrol bought in a cheaper area.

Shell International Petroleum publish a list, updated every March, of fuel prices and octane ratings for their products in every country where they sell fuel.

You must allow for the cost of oil replenishment and changes and other regular vehicle maintenance, plus the cost of roadside repairs such as punctures.

Third Party insurance for many African and Asian countries is not available from British insurance companies and often has to be bought at borders. It is usually compulsory but always strongly advisable. Premiums vary from country to country. Road tolls (mainly in Afghanistan, France, Italy and Spain) and ferry fares for the Straits of Gibraltar and river crossings on the African route must be covered.

The most likely unexpected costs are vehicle repair charges, and it is sensible to make a contingency allowance related to distance covered. An additional fund of 40 per cent of distance-related costs is suggested for this purpose.

Costs related to time

These consist mainly of food and accommodation. Prices in India and western Asia are about 50 per cent lower than in Europe, while in Africa, particularly the French-speaking areas, they may be nearly double the European level.

Economies can be made by sleeping in the vehicle, or camping, thus avoiding hotels and hostels, and by varying self-catering with the occasional meal at a small restaurant or tea house. Careful buying of local foods is a cost-saver provided you are able to choose suitable items, and if your vehicle is large enough you can set off with a good supply of canned and packaged foods.

Reserves

Apart from maintaining an adequate reserve to cope with

breakdowns, allowance must be made for other unexpected expenses due to illness, theft, accident, or miscalculation or misjudgement in the original estimate. You can insure against some of these misfortunes, and certainly should do so, but there is generally no way of getting immediate compensation. The suggested 40 per cent of distance-related costs is a minimum, and it is best to take more cash if you can, perhaps banking further funds that could be called on in an emergency. Otherwise, discuss with your bank manager the possibility of establishing 'rescue' facilities to a predetermined amount.

Two typical costings: Africa and Asia

The costings relate to hypothetical but typical journeys. They are intended to provide rough practical examples related to the main overlanders' continents. Prices are realistic at the time of writing, but allowance must be made for increases if an actual trip is costed on the basis suggested here.

No allowance is shown for buying the vehicle, a cost which is variable and may even be avoidable if you already have a suitable machine. Other variable or optional costs that have been omitted relate to buying new tyres, camping gear, maps and guide books, medical kit, postage, telephone and travel at the planning stage. Individuals must budget for souvenirs, presents, film, entertainments and hotel expenses: the analysis covers basic subsistence only.

The figures are based on trips of 16,000 miles in 90 days; trips to India or East Africa and back would be possible on this basis. The vehicle is a diesel-engined Land-Rover which should do at least 22mpg across Asia and 20mpg in the more difficult conditions across Africa.

A. *Pre-departure costs (1974/5 price levels)*

		Asia £	Africa £
Vehicle	tools	10	20
Costs	spare parts	25	40
	overhaul (materials only)	10	10
	AA or RAC membership	7	7
	carnet de passage	3	3
	insurance green card	15	15
	Channel ferry (return)	30	30
		100	125

		Asia £	Africa £
Costs	passport	6	6
per	visas	3	10
person	int. driving licence	1	1
	personal insurance	10	15
	misc. personal items	5	10
	Channel ferry (return)	10	10
		35	52

TOTALS   Asia: £100 + £35 per person
               Africa: £125 + £52 per person

B. *Costs related to distance (16,000 miles)*

	Asia	Africa
Fuel (diesel) @ 30p/gall in Asia, 60p in Africa	220	480
Oil changes and maintenance	30	40
Punctures and small repairs	25	40
Road tolls, ferries and border insurance	25	40
	300	600
Contingency allowance 40%	120	240
TOTALS	420	840

C. *Costs related to time (90 days)*

	Asia	Africa
Food @ 70p/day in Asia and £1.50 in Africa	63	135
Camp sites or other accommodation	10	10
Admission to places of interest	3	6
Postage and postcards home	2	2
TOTALS (per person)	78	153

Overall Costs (A + B + C)
  Asia: £520 + £113 per person
  Africa: £965 + £205 per person

The analysis shows that there are two major cost elements: first, the fixed cost related to the vehicle and distance travelled, usually shared by all participants; second, an additional cost per head. The larger the party, the smaller the fixed cost share per person; the following table shows the relationship of cost to size of party on the basis of the analysis just given:

	Asia £	Africa £
2 people	373 each	687 each
4	243	446
6	200	366
8	178	326
10	165	301

When preparing your own analysis you should investigate the probable cost of each item listed here, but in relation to your particular trip. Even if you plan to use a diesel **Land-Rover** for a 16,000-mile journey across Africa or Asia, do not blindly follow these figures or fail to take into consideration the variable or optional costs mentioned earlier. The cost of fuel will be one of the main variables, and the following table shows how greatly this can vary with different consumption rates and fuel prices. Note how fuel could be a small part of the overall cost with an economical vehicle in cheap fuel areas, or a very large component with a thirsty machine where fuel cost is high.

Fuel consumption/cost comparison over 16,000 miles

		Average cost per gall (pence)				
		20	30	50	80	100
Average	10	£320	480	800	1,280	1,600
consumption	20	£160	240	400	640	800
(mpg)	30	£107	160	270	428	540
	40	£ 80	120	200	320	400

1 gallon (UK) is approximately 4.5 litres

FINDING AND CHOOSING COMPANIONS

The cheapest way of going on an overland journey, apart from hitch-hiking, walking or cycling, is to join a large party. However, if you would prefer to travel in a small group, it is probably best to be ambitious as the trip will cost a lot anyway; so much of the cost relates to equipment that you get the best value for money by travelling for as long as possible outside Europe. The cost per mile or per day decreases the further and longer you travel; although India is twice as far as Turkey it does not cost twice as much to get there. If you are in a large group the high initial costs are shared by more people, but conditions are usually less comfortable and you may tire sooner. So either go with a large party on a cheap, shortish trip or plan well ahead for an elaborate long-distance journey-of-a-lifetime with a small group.

If you are organising a large group, the first problem is to find other passengers. The best method (in the UK) is to advertise in *Exchange & Mart*, the *Geographical Magazine*, *The Observer*, *Private Eye*, *The Sunday Times*, or *The Times*. The national papers will accept adverts only if you satisfy them that you are not out to make a profit and that you are 'respectable'. If you are at college or university, or a member of a club, you could advertise in its periodical or on notice boards.

It is important to ensure that members will get on well with one another. They should meet at an early stage, before committing themselves. The common interest of wanting to go on a self-organised trip is usually enough, but be cautious of great differences in age, personality or attitude.

Commercial overland trips

If you have never been on an overland trip before, or want to go at short notice and have limited time, or if you simply want to avoid the problems of organising your own journey, you would do well to choose a commercially organised tour. There are many overland tour operators, most of them based in the UK, and they tend to advertise in the 'Overland' columns of the *Geographical Magazine*, *The Observer*, *Private Eye*, *The Sunday Times*, and *Time Out*. At least two travel agencies specialise in overland travel: Trail Finders and Link Travel both of London. Trail Finders offer vehicles for charter and will, for a fee, give detailed, up-to-date advice on road conditions in Africa or Asia. Both agencies, and some operators, give film shows from time to time. Entrance is normally free, and they are worth seeing.

METHODS OF TRAVEL

Walking
The great Victorian explorers such as Livingstone, Burton and Speke walked most of the thousands of miles they covered. There has recently been renewed interest in marathon walks in Britain and the United States, and walker/writers such as John Hillaby and Eric Newby have amply described long-

distance walking in Africa and Asia. The potential walker—who is not necessarily a super-fit fanatic—will find his most useful guidance in the books of those who have already made long journeys on foot.

Hitch-hiking

Hitch-hiking is the cheapest practical method of travel. Outside Europe, most lorry drivers expect a small payment in return for a ride and passengers often have to travel on top or in the back in the dust, sun and rain; it is not usually a comfortable means of travel. Further disadvantages are that you must follow routes frequented by other traffic and cannot carry much with you. You are more at the mercy of officials, who usually take a dim view of this sort of travelling. The risk of illness is greater as hitch-hikers must eat and drink what is available during roadside halts.

Public transport

Bus travel in Africa, Asia and Latin America is usually cheap. Buses may carry chickens and goats as well as excessive numbers of passengers, but 'luxury' buses are sometimes available and are worth the extra expense if they allow a complete seat with a window. In some countries, bad driving makes bus journeys hazardous; this is particularly true in mountainous areas with sparse traffic.

There are few areas outside Europe with comprehensive railway networks. Most lines are single-track and many are narrow gauge, so trains tend to be slow and infrequent. Latin America shares with India the benefit of an extensive railway system and fares cheap enough to offer an attractive form of transport.

In Africa, boats ply the rivers Zaïre, Nile and Niger and lakes such as Victoria, Tanganyika and Malawi. These are often, but not always, cheap and invariably offer a fascinating journey. Many river and lake steamers carry cars, but shipping costs for vehicles can be high. The easiest way to reach Timbuctoo is on a Niger river steamer from Gao.

Your own vehicle

This book is intended mainly for the traveller in this category, who is ensured of completely independent travel. Although almost anything on wheels can be pressed into service, most overlanders use minibuses or Land-Rovers. Ordinary cars, motorbikes, scooters, mopeds and even bicycles have been used for major journeys.

CHOOSING A VEHICLE

If you are planning to stay on well-maintained tar roads, which you can do if you restrict yourself to going no further than North Africa or the Middle East or if you follow the one good through-route to India, then most 'soft' modern vehicles would be suitable. But if you want more freedom in your choice of routes, a more robust machine is essential. When going trans-Africa or exploring remote areas, it is best to use a cross-country vehicle, preferably with 4-wheel drive. Overloading is the most common cause of serious breakdowns, so it is important to be realistic and get a machine powerful enough for the job. As well as fuel and luggage there will be spare parts, camping equipment, food, water, oil and perhaps extra fuel to carry.

Diesel or petrol

Many types of minibus, as well as Land-Rovers, vans and even some cars are available with a choice of petrol or diesel engines. Most lorries and buses, world-wide, use diesel, so diesel fuel is generally at least as easy to get as petrol. Many people hesitate to use a diesel vehicle because the fuel injection equipment has a reputation for being unrepairable if it goes wrong. The mechanism is certainly complex, but provided the fuel injection pump is in good condition and maintenance of fuel filters is correctly and reliably carried out, the chances of system failure are slight; if the worst happens, most countries have facilities for overhauling injection pumps so repairs are not necessarily difficult to arrange. Diesels are widely used by commercial operators because they are much more reliable in operation than petrol engines, and the author's experiences with petrol and diesel Land-Rovers have borne this out. The outstanding advantage of the diesel on an overland trip is that it can be around one-third more economical than a comparable petrol engine; diesel fuel in many countries is half the price of petrol, and as a result a diesel can lower the fuel costs of an overland journey. Apart from the cost advantage, the diesel's greater economy means that less fuel needs to be carried in cans when crossing remote areas, so the loaded weight of the vehicle can be reduced. Diesel fuel is difficult to ignite, making the fire risk very slight, and a diesel vehicle can keep going after a complete electrical failure or with a wet engine (it has no ignition system). There is much to be said for its overland use.

This catalogue of advantages is intended mainly to redress the balance in favour of a type of engine that is so often maligned as an option for private use, but of course it has shortcomings. Size for size, a diesel engine is heavier, more expensive to buy (at least when new), less powerful and slower-revving than a petrol unit. A diesel Land-Rover may cruise at around 55 to 60mph while the equivalent petrol version will keep up a steady 65 to 70mph. The diesel is much noisier, especially at speed, so diesel users must pay for their lower fuel costs by having to shout to carry on a conversation. Sound-proofing felt helps. Diesel fuel is much messier than petrol, although spilled petrol is far more dangerous.

If you have to choose between petrol and diesel-powered vehicles, work out the saving from using a diesel and decide whether it is worthwhile. If you choose a diesel, make sure it is in good condition before you leave; if in doubt, fit an exchange injection pump and reconditioned injectors, and as this could be expensive bear it in mind when comparing the economics.

4-wheel drive

Vehicles in this category are invariably tough as they are designed for cross-country operation. They are less likely than most machines to give mechanical trouble and will stand up to abuse such as overloading, bumps, scrapes and other accidents that could seriously damage an ordinary vehicle. All have good ground clearance and will negotiate soft sand, mud, floods and snowdrifts. They are relatively expensive to buy and run, have heavy controls, an uncomfortable ride, and some have poor road-holding.

The Land-Rover is best-known and widely used for ambitious overland trips by private and commercial operators, and it is appropriate to describe its advantages and disadvantages in detail. The pros and cons of Land-Rover options such as short or long wheelbase, hard or soft top, petrol or diesel, can be applied in general to other vehicles with similar options.

A major consideration when choosing any vehicle is spare part availability. Here, the Land-Rover scores high as versions have been in production since 1948 and it is manufactured under licence in several countries of Africa and Asia. It is widely used by international agencies such as the UN, by the governments of many desert countries, and by a lot of armies. Spare parts are readily available through a comprehensive world-wide dealership and also (much cheaper) through bazaars, breakers' yards, scrap-dealers and military-surplus mongers in many places. The wide use of this vehicle by governments of sandy countries is a testimony to its suitability in off-the-road desert conditions.

The Land-Rover is available in short (88in) or long (109in) wheelbase. There have been three series, I, II and III. The first was built from 1948 to 1958 and many examples are still around (most of the taxis in Darjeeling are, to this day, early series Is). Series II came out in 1958, series IIa around 1961, and series III in 1971. Present Land-Rovers are offered with 4-cylinder and 6-cylinder petrol engines, and a 4-cylinder diesel. The bodies are aluminium alloy, which is strong, light and cannot rust. The simplest form is a pick-up truck with a canvas roof. At the other end of the scale, the 12-seater estate car or Safari model has four side-doors, sliding windows and a double-skinned tropical roof. This is the most useful version for overland travel but is the most expensive to buy. Caravan conversions with optional lifting roofs, cookers, refrigerators, cupboards and beds are made by specialist coachbuilders. Hard tops can be bought to replace canvas tilts.

The 'one ton' Land-Rover is a tougher version of the already fairly tough ordinary model. It has bigger tyres to cope with softer going and will carry a ton of payload across country. It is low-geared and therefore a little slower than other models. The tall, upright forward-control Land-Rover recently went out of production. It resembles a small lorry but uses the same basic chassis and machinery as other Land-Rovers. Although fairly rare, it is mentioned as the author's favourite overland vehicle and one on which he built a caravan conversion, choosing it because its forward-control cab allowed sufficient space for a caravan big enough to move around in. A new forward-control model is available only to military buyers at present; it is powered by a V8 petrol engine and promises to be fast and expensive.

Choice of wheelbase is important. Short models have the advantage of being less expensive, new and secondhand, and they are cheaper to ship since freight costs are usually calculated on the length or volume of a vehicle. They are generally more manoeuvrable and easier to handle, a point in their favour in mountainous areas. They usually have better acceleration and use slightly less fuel than the long model, but they are not such good overland vehicles because they have less space in the back, are almost impossible to sleep in (unless a special shelf is built projecting over the front seats), and give a less comfortable ride (they are prone to fore-and-aft pitching on uneven roads). On corrugated dirt roads, mud or other loose surfaces, short vehicles lack directional stability compared with long ones and can easily spin off the road.

Canvas-roofed models are cheaper, new and secondhand, but are not advised for an overland trip. The tropical sun is usually far too strong to drive with the canvas removed and the contents of the vehicle are vulnerable to theft; anyone can cut the canvas or undo the securing straps. Canvas rots and tears after a surprisingly short time in tropical sunlight and is expensive to replace. Plastic windows in the canvas become scratched and opaque after a short time on dusty roads. A canvas top is best changed for a metal or fibreglass roof. The conversion is simple.

The estate car Land-Rovers have a double-skinned tropical

roof which offers two main advantages: people can safely walk around on top, so the roof can be used as an observation platform as well as a luggage carrier; it keeps the inside of the vehicle cooler in strong sun and warmer at night or in winter. It is fairly easy to fit a home-made tropical roof to any single-skinned roof.

There are a number of other 4-wheel-drive vehicles, some of which are better in certain respects than Land-Rovers, but none has the same world-wide spares availability although a few rival or better the Land-Rover in specific areas.

One of the Land-Rover's rivals is the Range Rover, a tough 4-wheel-drive car. It is much faster and more comfortable than a Land-Rover but is only to be considered by the wealthier overlander, because of its high initial price and heavy fuel consumption.

The Toyota Land-Cruiser is perhaps the Land-Rover's most serious rival. This steel-bodied Japanese machine is similar in many respects, but is slightly bigger and has a much more powerful petrol engine (6-cylinder, 3·9 litre). It is therefore faster and not much less economical overall. Spares are available in East and Southern Africa, Australia, and also in parts of Europe and Asia. Hard- and soft-top versions, and an estate car variant, are produced.

Most American car manufacturers produce 4-wheel-drive pick-up trucks, usually big, powerful and thirsty. They are more sophisticated than most European or Japanese 4-wheel-drive vehicles, with power steering and sometimes automatic transmission, and are worth considering if finance is no problem and you are prepared to carry a lot of spare parts, often impossible to get in parts of Africa, Asia and even Europe.

Continental Europe produces a number of 4-wheel-drive vehicles, the lightest, smallest and most economical of which is the Austrian Haflinger. It is rather slow (maximum speed about 50mph), but will go through the most impossible-looking terrain. The Germans produce the Mercedes Unimog, a highly specialised cross-country vehicle, very expensive to buy, and much better than the average overlander needs.

If the party is large (between twelve and twenty), the best

value for money in large 4×4 vehicles, at least in the UK, is an ex-army Bedford RL. These are sometimes advertised in *Exchange & Mart* and are sold at army auction sales. Sales at Ruddington Ordnance Storage Depot near Nottingham are held every few months. Ex-army RLs are usually petrol-engined but can readily be converted to diesel power, with a consequent improvement in consumption from 6 or 8mpg to about 14mpg. Many civilian RLs are converted models, and these occasionally come up for sale. Other ex-army 4×4s such as Humbers and Austins are available at military auctions. Spares are usually reasonably easy to get and the Bedford range of trucks has a good reputation for reliability. An obsolete British 4×4 vehicle still occasionally seen is the Austin Gipsy; it looks rather like a Land-Rover. Although most Gipsy owners are enthusiastic about the vehicle, spares are impossible to find outside the UK.

The World War II jeep makes a good overland machine if well-maintained. It is now old and rare enough to be appreciating in value, an unusual point in its favour. Another ex-military 4-wheel-drive vehicle, commonly found in the UK but also sold in small numbers by the British army in both Holland and Germany, is the Austin Champ, an elaborate type of jeep designed for the British army and powered by a Rolls Royce-designed engine. Champs are complicated machines and if not well-maintained can be unreliable; their back-axles have a reputation for being troublesome. The Champ and the Jeep both have canvas tops and limited carrying capacity and neither is recommended for overland trips unless at least one of the party understands how to maintain and repair the vehicle. The British army is replacing its Champs with Land-Rovers, which explains why many Champs are available on the civilian market.

2-wheel drive

Possibly only ten miles in ten thousand will call for 4-wheel drive. A 2-wheel-drive vehicle is adequate for most journeys but it must be robust and have good ground clearance. Mini-buses are probably the most useful and commonly used means of overland transport; they are reasonably comfortable, economical to run, and can easily be converted into caravans. Volkswagen produce some of the most popular overland minibuses; current models are the Caravette, which is a ready-built caravan and can be ordered with a lifting roof, the Microbus (a 12-seater bus), a range of closed vans called Transporters which are suitable for conversion into caravans, and the Kombi, another version of the minibus. VWs have medium-power petrol engines. Ground clearance is better than average and the general quality is high; elderly secondhand ones can be found in well-preserved condition. The rear-engined layout gives good traction in sand and mud.

This reputation has led many VW owners to take their vehicles alone into areas which are inadvisable for any but 4-wheel-drive machines, and the frequent abandoned wrecks of this make in remote parts of the Sahara testify to the foolhardiness of over-ambitious travellers. However, for all except the most difficult areas the VW is an ideal overland vehicle, being tough and reliable and having good world-wide spares availability. Volkswagen in Great Britain will supply VW owners with a useful booklet of advice on operating their vehicles in tropical climates.

Volkswagens suffer from two main shortcomings, both of which can and should be guarded against. First: their engines are inclined to overheat in dusty and hot conditions; if this is allowed to continue, irreparable damage could result. The cost of a replacement engine in, for example, India, would be over £500, and there would be a long delay. The most common cause is either loss of oil (the oil helps to cool the engine) or dust and dirt clogging the cooling fins, which is more likely to happen if there are oil leaks. Three simple and effective precautions against this are to keep the cooling fins clean and check them frequently, to prevent oil leaks and keep the oil well topped-up in hot running conditions, and to give yourself warning of overheating by fitting a temperature gauge and *watching it*. The author knows of many cases where people neglected their VW engines in hot conditions and had to write them off completely. Second (and less common): an engine fire can quickly reach the fuel tank. Guard against this by keeping the carburettor in good condition and carrying two fire extinguishers. It should be possible to fix a fire-warning device in the engine compartment.

Ford Transits are available with petrol or diesel engines and come in normal and long wheelbase models. Spares are generally obtainable in most developed countries. Twelve-seater petrol Transits are manufactured in Turkey as well as the UK and Germany. Many overland companies run the big 13- and 17-seaters. A range of caravan conversions is available. A good, cheap alternative is the older Thames, which needs to be checked carefully for rust.

Bedford, the UK General Motors' subsidiary, has produced minibuses for some years, and the current CF range includes big- and small-bodied variants with petrol or diesel engines and caravan conversions, and the older 3-geared Utilabrake is a popular buy for those wanting a cheaper vehicle. Mechanical and body condition must be checked.

British Leyland produce two series of vans, the J4 and the 250JU. The J4 is smaller, cheaper and more economical than either its stablemate or the Fords and Bedfords. Both British Leyland machines come with petrol or diesel engines, and caravan conversions are available.

Commer, the Chrysler UK subsidiary, produce a van that serves as a basis for the successful Highwayman motorised caravan which has completed a number of well-publicised round-the-world and other long-distance trips.

A point to beware of with all minibuses: they are easily overloaded because they have so much space.

Cars and small vans

For smaller parties, cars or small vans can be adequate. If you intend travelling off hard roads for any great distance, choose a tough machine with larger-than-average wheels and good ground clearance. Pseudo-cross-country vehicles like the Volkswagen VW 181, the British Leyland Mini-Moke or beach buggies are less suitable than the conventional vehicles from which they are derived. The overlander should, if he needs an off-the-road vehicle, get one properly designed for the job.

A few cars and vans stand out as having advantages in strength, ground clearance or spares availability. Volkswagens, Peugeots and some Fords are tough, reliable and have a good world-wide spares service. Citroën's Deux Chevaux (2cv) and the Renault 4 are hard to beat for petrol economy, and though the 2cv has a ride like a small boat in a rough sea it copes well with uneven surfaces. The British Leyland Mini series can be useful; what they lose in poor ground clearance they gain in having a small overhang front and back, and they are economical; the Mini-van is cheap to buy and can, at a pinch, sleep two.

As always when buying an older vehicle, check body condition. Rough roads may cause a rust-weakened body literally to fall apart.

Motorised caravans

The best overland transport for two or three people is a motorised caravan, with its built-in beds, gas cooker and cupboards, and perhaps a refrigerator, shower and chemical toilet. A variety of professionally built models is available, but it is possible to buy the fittings and convert a van or minibus yourself. Ideally, you should be able to sleep, cook and eat in a motorised caravan without having to get outside, but if there is not enough space you can often buy or make an extension awning which fixes to the vehicle. When buying a ready-made caravan conversion for an overland trip, check the fittings for robustness; all cupboards should be strong, with positive catches (spring ball catches are not good enough as they allow doors to fly open on rough roads).

Several firms make neat fibreglass lifting roofs with two bunks; they are easily raised and lowered and can be fitted to a wide variety of vehicles.

Motorcycles and scooters

Two-wheel transport is the most economical means for a solo traveller. Pillion riding for a trip as long as the average overland journey is not worth considering, although a sidecar offers a possibility for two. The main advantage of using a motorcycle or scooter is that fuel and shipping costs are low, so that, for example, a round-the-world trip becomes an economical proposition.

Motorcycles will go down narrow animal tracks and footpaths which no other vehicle can follow. The main disadvantages are the vulnerability of the rider in an accident, exposure to sun and dust, rain and snow, and the difficulty of carrying enough equipment and spares. A high degree of skill is needed to ride a motorcycle safely, particularly the skill to anticipate the behaviour of the vehicle on different surfaces, so only the most confident riders should attempt an overland trip. Most motorcycles or scooters are relatively highly stressed; a degree of mechanical understanding is therefore vital.

Motorcyclists will be refused access to the East African game reserves (as will travellers in other open vehicles).

Preparation

PAYING FOR YOUR TRIP

Abandon hope of financial sponsorship by companies; they have all been approached many times before. If you have an unusual purpose or destination some companies may supply a few free samples of their products, but most feel that overland trips do not have sufficient publicity value to justify greater generosity.

Having cut the costs of your overland journey by organising a large group, not being too ambitious, or by getting an economical vehicle, you can further reduce them by making it oneway, perhaps to or from a job in a distant country. If you are going to work, it is best to try and arrange employment before you leave as you will almost certainly need a work permit. However, in some places you can get casual jobs such as teaching English privately, proof-reading for English-language newspapers, or doing secretarial work for British or American companies. You can pick up paying passengers on your way; this is not recommended, but it can be useful if your budget has been hit by unexpectedly high expenses. You are not allowed to compete with local buses and taxis so you should never carry people locally within one country for money. Your insurance will not cover the carriage of paying passengers, although where cost-sharing ends and fare-paying begins may be hard to define. So long as your passengers are being carried in the remoter parts of the world, from one country to another, and are nationals of neither, and so long as they agree (preferably in writing) to travel at their own risk, you can be reasonably confident. It is easy to find passengers in Istanbul who want to go east towards Afghanistan or India or home across Europe, by putting up a notice in the Pudding Shop, a café near the Blue Mosque. Your prospective passengers are likely to be good, honest company, but you must be selective; a few promise to pay later and never do, and occasionally one will disappear with your money or your camera. Another hazard of carrying passengers first met on the journey (particularly in Nepal, Afghanistan and Morocco) is that they may be carrying drugs. The penalties are severe, and the driver is usually regarded as an accessory and his vehicle confiscated. Never carry parcels across borders on behalf of other people; if there are drugs inside, the customs officers will never believe your protestations of innocence.

Buying or selling is a possibility, but you will be competing with existing commercial operations. You can sometimes pay for repairs with tools or something else of value; the author once paid for a welding repair in the Sahara with his transistor radio at a very favourable exchange rate. However, people have been jailed in Turkey for selling a tin of coffee or a packet of razorblades and unknowingly evading duty, so be careful. Some overlanders sell their vehicles and fly home, but it is not usually possible to do this legally without paying a lot of duty. Travellers have sold vehicles without too much trouble in Nepal, Afghanistan, South Africa, Kenya and Kuwait, but you can never count on a successful sale.

A few people make money out of their journey by writing or photography, but unless well-established in these fields you will be fortunate to do so.

In Greece and some Middle Eastern countries it is possible to sell your blood, but this should be done not more than once every six months if resistance to infection is to be maintained.

Probably the only way to make enough money to more than cover your costs is to drive for a commercial overland organisation. You could drive either freight or passengers, but no established company will consider you unless you already have useful experience with the sort of vehicles they use. You cannot normally drive passengers unless you are at least 25, as insurance is not readily available to cover younger drivers. You will need a PSV (public service vehicle) licence to drive passengers commercially and an HGV (heavy goods vehicle) licence for lorries. As most overland freight is carried in 32-ton or larger articulated units, this job is available to a small minority of experienced long-distance truck drivers.

CARRYING MONEY

Travellers' cheques
The safest way of carrying large sums of money is in the form of travellers' cheques, which are easy to cash all over the world, not only in banks but often in hotels, shops, tourist offices, and at the exchange offices found at many major frontier crossings. It is best to obtain cheques in the smallest possible denominations as this allows greater flexibility in the amounts you can cash. Travellers' cheques usually cost 1 per cent of face value, and you may have to pay commission when you change them. You can buy cheques in almost any hard currency and may find it useful to carry an assortment of currencies. Their main advantage is that if they are lost or stolen they are usually replaceable. If you lose your cheques, report the loss to the nearest police authority immediately and try to get a written statement from them confirming the circumstances of the loss. Then inform the nearest agency representing your brand of cheques, or cable details to the issuing bank or office. Always keep a separate note of the numbers, and cross them off as you cash the cheques. If you cannot give the issuing office the numbers of lost cheques there may be a delay in replacing them or, in some circumstances, it may not be possible to recoup the loss. A disadvantage is that travellers' cheques are often exchanged at a slightly less favourable rate than cash, and are not always changed as easily as cash in shops and bazaars.

Cash

Cash is liable to be lost or stolen. Travellers' baggage insurance will usually cover the loss of a certain amount of cash and you can insure against the loss of larger amounts, but compensation is not easily obtained until you return home.

Dollar bills are useful if you are short of local currency, as they are recognised and accepted almost everywhere. When driving in the Sahara and other French-speaking parts of Africa, carry about £50 in French 100fr and 10fr notes to cope with unexpected emergencies. Your supply of French francs can usually be replenished at banks in Mali, Ivory Coast and Senegal at a good exchange rate.

The currency of most Asian, African and Eastern European countries is often accepted only at a bad exchange rate outside the country of issue. Many countries prohibit the export of their currency or allow it to be taken out in small amounts only, so it is wise to obtain no more local currency than you are likely to need because you will always lose when changing it back. Keep all bank or exchange office receipts in such countries, as you will often be asked to produce them (to prove you have changed money legally) when you want to change local money back to hard currency.

Your bank or travel agent will tell you how much in sterling, travellers' cheques and foreign banknotes can be taken out of the UK. If you feel that the permitted amount will be insufficient, you should ask your bank manager about obtaining Bank of England clearance for an increase.

Coins are a nuisance; banks happily issue them but nearly always refuse to take them in exchange for a foreign currency. This happens even at borders and on some cross-Channel ferries where they could easily be reissued to people going in the opposite direction. It pays to spend all coins before you leave a country.

It is often useful to obtain in advance a little of the currency of each of the countries you will pass through so that you have enough to buy a meal or some food if you arrive after the banks have closed or on a public holiday, when it is difficult to change money. Some countries have no exchange facilities on their borders and you have to drive to the first big town (which may be hundreds of miles from the frontier in Saharan countries) before you can get local money. British banks usually give a bad exchange rate when they sell obscure currencies so do not buy more than you need. Some countries allow you to bring in only a limited amount of their currency, so check the regulations with your bank; the excess may be confiscated if you take too much. The Swiss banks operate an international free currency market and can sometimes offer currency at better rates than apply in the country of issue.

Free and black markets

In some countries, money can be exchanged in the bazaars at a better rate than in the banks. This is sometimes legal but more often not. Overlanders are soon made aware of the situation by touts who pursue them with exhortations to 'Change money, mistah.' It is not unknown for customs officers to help travellers with their currency exchange problems and probably make themselves the price of a packet of cigarettes into the bargain, and it is generally true to say that small-scale manipulation to save the odd dollar or two is overlooked by the authorities, but you should never count on it. Most black market deals are illegal and carry a degree of risk.

The main chance of getting caught arises from money-changing touts who may also be police informers and, in addition, have a variety of ways of cheating the unwary traveller by short-changing him, giving him counterfeit money, or robbing him by trickery or violence. Most overlanders at some stage change money in the bazaars and back streets of the east. If you are involved in such a situation, try to choose your own place for the transaction; if you have to go to a back street shop, don't go alone; do not carry more cash than you want to change or hand over money or travellers' cheques until the dealer has clearly counted out the agreed amount of local currency and a straight swap is possible. Most private money-changers are reasonably straight with the people they deal with or they would go out of business, and the risks are not enormous, but if you are caught do not expect sympathy from the police. You should watch out for unusually clean or large-denomination notes as these may be forgeries; insist on well-used smaller denominations, but untorn, as torn banknotes are often rejected by shopkeepers.

Afghanistan is a major free market because currency transactions there by private individuals are legal. Kabul usually gives a better rate than the provincial towns, and Indian and Pakistani rupees can be bought there at a favourable rate although they are not supposed to be taken into Pakistan or India.

Shop around to get the best rate; never accept the first offer, always haggle. Be suspicious of an unbelievably good offer as it is sometimes a ploy used by dishonest touts to work a trick such as counting out a pile of high-denomination notes which, apart from the top few, all turn out to be low, or folding notes in half and counting each half as a separate note.

All currency transactions, whether in a bank or the back room of a curio shop, seem to take a long time once you leave Europe. Banks in most countries type an exchange form in quadruplicate and get a different official to sign each copy. The whole procedure can take an hour.

Newsweek magazine carries a table of official and unofficial exchange rates, and travellers coming the other way can give up-to-date information on where best to change your money.

Keeping your money safely

Many travellers wear a broad leather money belt which is a discreet and reasonably safe way of carrying it. The author usually has a lockable box (a cash box is ideal) bolted somewhere out of sight in his vehicle to hold documents and cash. If drilling holes in the floor to secure a box, take care that brake and fuel pipes are not damaged. Use mushroom-headed bolts, heads inside, and self-locking nuts below the vehicle. Plastic wallets of the sort given away free by most banks are used to carry a small supply of ready cash, and bank cash-envelopes are useful for keeping coins; it is a good idea to keep coins and notes for different countries in different envelopes. Cash or vital documents should never be kept in suitcases or personal luggage, which are most vulnerable to theft.

KEEPING TRACK OF COSTS

It is important to keep a daily record of expenditure, and to keep an eye on the overall budget to ensure that the money will last the trip. A treasurer should have responsibility for this, but if no person willingly accepts the task an account-keeping rota should be organised.

Avoid complicated accounting systems. The big expenses will generally be associated with running the vehicle and should be noted in a record book listing all fuel and oil purchases, repairs and spare parts. The date, place and mileage reading for each transaction are best kept in a notebook on the dashboard, handy for instant use. Expenses should be recorded immediately. It is useful to add information such as the mileage reading at the start of each day so that progress can be checked.

Individual members should keep personal records of eating and living expenses and details of travellers' cheques cashed.

A large group will probably find it worth organising a kitty to cover joint expenses such as the cost of camp-cooked food, gas refills, camp site fees and so on, and someone should keep a kitty book and organise a whip-round when funds need replenishing.

It is best not to use kitty funds for anything other than joint expenditure from which each member benefits equally.

PERSONAL DOCUMENTS

Passport

UK citizens must use the full (dark blue, gilded) document, available from any passport office. The cheaper Visitor's Passport is useless outside Europe. Application forms are obtainable from major travel agencies, some banks and employment exchanges, as well as passport offices. It can take three weeks to issue or renew a passport, although the office will sometimes speed things up in cases of genuine urgency.

All countries outside Europe stamp passports on entry and exit, but in remote areas such as the Sahara almost every préfecture in every small oasis will insist on making its mark.

If you need a replacement passport during the trip,

because the original has been filled, it must be obtained from the nearest embassy or consulate representing your country.

The life of a passport is prolonged if officials can be discouraged from putting small exit and entry stamps in the middle of a clean page; they will usually find a corner of a used page if asked. The British ten-year passport has too few pages, and a welcome innovation is the 'jumbo' passport with over twice as many visa pages; it also costs twice as much. United States citizens are lucky, as any American embassy can add extra pages to a full passport, even at short notice.

Visas

The trend at present is to make travel easier, and a number of countries have relaxed their requirements. UK citizens travelling overland to India need visas for Iran, Afghanistan and Pakistan. Africa is more complicated. Citizens of Commonwealth countries generally do not need visas for other Commonwealth countries, although some have retaliated against Britain's immigration regulations by insisting on entry permits instead. In any case, it is wise to check with the embassies of all countries you plan to visit.

Some visa applications have to be supported by 'proof of sufficient funds', which can take the form of a letter from your bank. A few Arab states ask for a 'baptismal certificate', which could be provided by a minister of religion. Countries with religious establishments can be difficult towards people who claim to be atheists; South Africa and several Arab countries come within this category.

If you are offered the option of getting your visa at a border, never count on it unless you have up-to-date and reliable information that it is possible. No immigration officer will let you in without the correct visa, no matter how much you argue or plead. A visa obtained at the point of entry may cost more than it would had it been bought at an embassy.

Visas can be got en route from the appropriate embassies in other capital cities than your own, but one or two countries insist on visas or entry permits issued in your own country.

The price of visas varies and some are free. Before you apply for a visa, find out what kinds are available, how long they last and what they cost. You can save trouble by making sure that a visa gives you more than enough time to cross the country, because obtaining extensions is at best a nuisance and at worst impossible. Transit visas usually allow one entry and one exit with perhaps a week or sometimes fifteen days in between. Entry visas often run for three months. Multiple entry visas (which are usually expensive) allow you to go in and out of a country several times. Many visas must be used within a certain period, and should not be obtained too early if this is the case.

The visas and stamps in a passport will show immigration officers where you have been or are going, and many countries will refuse to let you in if you are on your way to an enemy country. At the time of writing, an Israeli stamp will bar you from all Arab states. Similarly, Rhodesian stamps or a South African visa could well prevent entry into many countries in the rest of Africa. To circumvent problems of this nature, it is sometimes possible to get a second passport where an itinerary has forced the collection of conflicting visas.

If trying to get visas in a hurry, it helps to go personally to the embassies concerned. It is worth dressing neatly as embassy staff sometimes seem to resent travellers who look as if they are hard up, while they often appear to make efforts to speed up visa applications, and may be less likely to ask for proof of sufficient funds, if an applicant looks affluent (even if he isn't).

International driving licence

All intending drivers will need this document, which is normally obtainable only from national motoring organisations or the government department in the country which issued the driver's national licence.

In the UK, the AA and RAC will issue international licences to holders of full British licences. Application is made on a special form with provision for two passport-size photographs (machine photographs are acceptable).

International vaccination certificate

All travellers will need proof of vaccination against smallpox and usually cholera also. Visitors to tropical Africa and parts of Latin America require a yellow fever vaccination certificate. (A later section deals specifically with vaccinations.)

Camping carnet

A permit to camp may be required; it is not expensive. You should ask representatives of the countries to be visited whether it is needed.

VEHICLE DOCUMENTS

A vehicle registered in the UK will have a registration book, insurance certificate and possibly a roadworthiness certificate. It is wise, though not essential, to carry these documents, because it sometimes pays to present to officials the fullest documentation possible.

You are not required to show a valid licence disc once you leave the UK and can claim a refund for the unexpired months on a paid-up licence.

Carnet de passage

Most countries outside Europe require this document, which is issued by the national motoring organisations. They guarantee the government of a country for which the carnet is valid payment in full of any customs duty, or fines for illegal importation, if the vehicle is illicitly sold or otherwise disposed of in the territory. The organisations will want to reclaim payments from the document-holder, and usually demand solid security before they will issue a carnet. This generally takes the form of a banker's guarantee of compensation, for which the bank may also require security.

It is possible to insure against a claim, but rarely worth it as the premium is high when a high level of security is demanded, while a banker's guarantee is usually easy to get if a low level is required. The amount of security needed depends on the countries to be visited and on the rates of duty or fines they impose when vehicles are not re-exported. It might be about half the value of the vehicle, or (as in the case of Iran which, at the time of writing, has about the highest rates of duty), as much as 300 per cent of the value of the vehicle when *new*. In other words, security of the order of several thousand pounds could be required for a carnet, against a house or large paid-up assurance policy in the absence of substantial money reserves.

If the vehicle is not sold, stolen or abandoned, the need for compensation never arises. If the vehicle is burnt out, wrecked, or otherwise written off, the authorities will usually clear the carnet, having first checked that the engine, chassis and registration numbers tally. Clearly, it pays to avoid exaggerating the value of the vehicle when applying for a carnet.

As the vehicle can never be in more than one country at a time, the security needed will be governed by the highest rate of duty charged on your route (the Iranian authorities, it is fair to mention, will occasionally issue a temporary import permit which drastically reduces the security demanded).

When applying for a carnet, complete all details relating to the vehicle with great care and accuracy. If a vehicle has been fitted with a new engine at some stage, the number may not tally with that on the registration book; this must be rectified. Customs officers sometimes check carnets against vehicles, and it is at times like this that earlier care will pay off.

When the carnet arrives, ensure that the details have been correctly transcribed from the application form.

Each page of the carnet de passage is perforated to give two tear-off strips plus a counterfoil. All information is repeated on each of the three parts. The first strip is removed by a customs officer when you enter a country, the second when you leave. The counterfoil, which remains in the book, should be stamped and initialled by a customs officer, once on entry and once on exit. The exit stamp is particularly important as it furnishes proof that you have removed the vehicle from the country and protects you against a claim for duty. The carnet de passage must be returned at the end of your trip to the issuing organisation; send it by registered post in view of its value.

A trailer is covered by a separate carnet.

Control documents for minibuses (EEC regulations)

If you cross Europe in a minibus or vehicle with ten or more seats (including the driver's) you have to conform to regulations which apply in EEC (European Economic Community) countries.

The driver must be over 21 and have held a full driving licence for at least one year; the proof required is a certificate from a traffic area office (UK) of the Department of the Environment. The department will tell you where your nearest office is and send an explanatory leaflet.

The driver must maintain a special control book while driving through EEC countries. As Britain is an EEC country, this regulation applies from the start of an international journey leaving any part of the UK. The control book is a record of the hours a driver spends at the wheel, and all driving and rest periods must be entered. Regulations cover the length of time it is permitted to drive at a stretch and lay down statutory breaks and daily maxima. A police officer may ask to inspect the record, and as the regulations are backed by stiff penalties for infringement it is best to organise this paperwork properly.

It is not necessary to keep records outside the EEC.

The control book is obtainable from traffic area offices, as is the last bureaucratic imposition, the journey control document.

VACCINATIONS

Up to three vaccinations may be compulsory: smallpox for almost everywhere, cholera for most of Asia and much of Africa, and yellow fever for most of equatorial Africa and Latin America. Requirements change, especially for cholera, depending on when and where outbreaks occur, and on balance it is best to be vaccinated and obtain certificates. Certain other vaccinations, not compulsory, are nevertheless advisable (see table opposite).

Certificates must remain valid for the entire period of your journey, or you will have to get boosters. A traveller without valid and relevant certificates can be held in quarantine for the incubation period of the disease.

	Effective after...	Effective (and cert valid) for...	Incubation period
smallpox*	8 days	3 years	4-16 days
cholera*	6 days	6 months	1-5 days
yellow fever*	10 days	10 years	6 days
paratyphoid	1 day	1 year	1-3 weeks
typhoid	1 day	1 year	1-3 weeks
tetanus+	1 day	5 years	2 days-6 months

* compulsory for many countries
+ 2 vaccinations needed, 4 weeks apart, and booster after 1 year

Some vaccinations can be combined as one dose to reduce the number of injections actually needed. Typhoid and paratyphoid are usually given together, and can be mixed with cholera or tetanus boosters. However, for medical reasons some have to be given several weeks apart, and timing is therefore a matter of planning. Most doctors can give all vaccinations except yellow fever, which is given only at certain centres. The Hospital for Tropical Diseases, in London, will provide a free course of vaccinations by appointment. There is usually a long waiting list, and it is advisable to make an appointment at least six weeks in advance and about ten or twelve weeks before departure. Vaccination for a fee can be arranged at short notice in London at the British Airways terminal medical department (Victoria) and the West London Vaccination Centre.

Overlanders starting outside the London area or from other countries should ask a doctor or the local department of health for advice about where to get vaccinations.

Wherever you get your vaccinations, make sure that you will be issued with the standard international certificates and that the correct sections are stamped and countersigned. A missing signature or stamp could result in your detention in quarantine, or revaccination.

The wise overlander arranges immunisation against poliomyelitis (usually an oral dose), visits his dentist for a check-up, and consults his doctor if he suffers from potentially troublesome ailments such as asthma or hay fever. People who wear glasses or contact lenses should carry a spare pair, and contact lens wearers would be wise to take glasses too as dust can cause irritation. A copy of the prescription for your lenses could prove useful if glasses have to be replaced en route.

INSURANCE

Personal cover

A standard travellers' package policy provides cover for medical expenses resulting from illness or accident, and loss of property and money. Medical cover is usually sold in units of £250, and at least two units at this rate should be bought for travel anywhere in the Americas where medical treatment is expensive. Compensation for accidents, morbidly costed at so much per limb or the cost of sending the remains home, is usually offered in £1,000 ($2,200) units and is worth getting. Baggage insurance covers loss of property and a certain amount of cash; single articles such as cameras which are worth more than a specified amount must often be declared separately, and you should find out if this is necessary before parting with a premium.

Make sure that cover will be valid in all countries to be visited (world-wide cover is best) and that it will run for the full length of your journey. It is easy to forget to renew it if it expires during the trip.

Vehicle insurance

Insurance cover in Europe can usually be obtained by an extension of a normal British vehicle policy; there will be an additional premium. Compulsory third party cover can be bought at frontiers but is usually expensive in Europe, and the transactions waste a lot of time.

British insurance companies are generally unable to settle third party claims in African or Asian countries due to exchange control difficulties. In a few cases they have local subsidiaries or arrangements with local companies, but third party cover must usually be bought at borders outside Europe. It is not always compulsory and sometimes cannot be arranged except at the first sizeable town, but third party cover is important as the consequences of even a minor accident when uninsured can be desperately serious. Travellers in such situations have been held in jail for long periods. If you have insurance (and the premium for a short period is generally low) you can normally count on the insurance company coming to your aid fairly quickly. Some countries, such as Algeria and Afghanistan, automatically levy an insurance premium on motorised travellers arriving at their borders.

Fire and theft, or fire, theft and accidental damage cover is best obtained through insurers in your own country; then, if you need to claim, you can be reasonably sure of getting compensation. Exchange control may prevent national insurance companies in African and Asian countries from sending out compensation if you insure locally. Insurance cover for vehicles outside Europe is a specialist business and most general vehicle insurance companies will not handle it. Cover usually has to be obtained from underwriters through a broker.

MAIL

Poste restante
The easiest way to collect mail during a long journey is to use the poste restante service available at all main post offices throughout the world. The correct way to address letters is: name of recipient, Poste Restante, Main Post Office *or* GPO (*in English-speaking areas*)/PTT (*in French-speaking areas*), town or city, country.

The post is usually filed according to the first letter of the recipient's surname, which can cause problems if the communication bears two or more of your names or if you have a double-barrelled family name. The convention of writing the family name last is not universal and it is a good idea to encourage people to address their letters with initials and surname only. It is also important that they write the first letter of your surname clearly and conventionally, particularly when sending letters to areas where Roman script is unfamiliar, such as most Islamic countries. It is often worth asking the clerk to check the pigeonholes labelled with the initial of your first names, and even E for Esq.

Telegrams and registered items are often kept separately and noted on a list, which you should ask the clerk to show you.

A small charge is payable for poste restante facilities in some countries.

The main advantage of poste restante is that it provides the quickest possible service. A disadvantage is that you can collect mail only when the post office is open. Some major centres open the poste restante counters in their main post offices for longer periods than the general counters, but as post offices usually observe all public holidays they may prove to be unexpectedly closed for the day.

Other places to collect mail

Mail can be sent to hotels and campsites or collected from American Express offices and some banks (if you are a user of their travellers' cheques).

Embassies will sometimes agree to hold post, but you should always write in advance for permission. British embassies in busy centres will generally ask you to use the poste restante service. A list of British embassies, high commissions and consulates can be obtained from the Foreign and Commonwealth Office in London.

Delivery time

Post to major capital cities on international air routes takes a few days only and rarely more than a week, except to distant places. Local postal services depend entirely on the efficiency of the local post office. Major cities such as Nairobi, Lagos, Tehran and Delhi enjoy a quick service.

The best plan is to ask people to post airletters at least one week before you are due in capital cities and perhaps ten days or a fortnight before you plan to arrive in lesser towns. If your schedule changes you can send back a revised itinerary. Poste restante is normally held for a month or more before being returned to the sender, so there is no harm in posting early.

Equipment

A ROOF OVER YOUR HEAD

The most practical arrangement for small groups is to sleep in the vehicle, which avoids the need for tents.

Tents should be small and light when collapsed, waterproof and insect-proof when up, well ventilated and quick to put up and take down. Cotton and canvas are not as good as synthetic materials such as nylon and PVC because they rot and lose their proofing in time. Small ridge tents are the least expensive and most compact accommodation, but be careful when choosing, as the cheapest type is often not sufficiently waterproof. A sewn-in groundsheet will keep out unpleasant bedfellows like scorpions, and a zip-up entrance with adequate netted ventilation will keep sleepers cool and free from mosquitoes. Several French firms make small ridge tents with cotton-muslin sides, a sewn-in PVC groundsheet and a nylon flysheet which will withstand a monsoon deluge. Some have rubber loops instead of adjustable guys and can be put up very quickly. Igloo tents with inflatable support tubes are quick to erect but become puncture-prone as they get older. Frame tents are bulky, expensive, and slow to assemble and dismantle.

Hardy travellers can consider using a waterproof sleeping bag and possibly lashing a tarpaulin to the side of the vehicle as extra cover, but should not sleep under the vehicle unless it is free of oil leaks. It is pleasant to sleep under the stars in desert conditions, but at high altitudes be prepared for a drastic drop in temperature once the sun goes down. Anyone planning to sleep in the open will find a space-blanket is a good investment; this product of the American space programme consists of a metal foil sheet, silver on one side and coloured on the other. Silver side inwards, it reflects body heat and retains warmth; coloured side in, heat is dispersed and the sleeper keeps cool. It is extremely light and folds up small, but would-be purchasers should make sure that they buy the reusable sort; some types can be used once only.

COOKING EQUIPMENT

In Asia, where roadside cafés and tea houses are frequent and cheap, you need only a small picnic stove with a single burner for brewing tea, coffee and soup, but a double-burner camping stove (or two single burners) will make it possible to prepare meals more varied than stews and fry-ups.

The most convenient type of cooker runs on propane or butane gas, but exchanging or refilling cylinders presents problems on overland trips. Other cookers use petrol (gasoline), paraffin (kerosene) or solid fuel pellets.

Gas cylinders (propane or butane)

Camping Gaz equipment is widely advertised and available from camping shops and camp sites all over Europe. They offer cookers that run on throw-away cartridges (which do not last long enough for an overland journey, necessitating the carriage of a large number of spares) and from exchangeable, refillable cylinders. The biggest cylinder holds 6lb of gas, is quite expensive, and impossible to exchange in most parts of Africa and Asia; it is generally filled with butane which will not vaporise readily in cool conditions, which causes difficulty if you are trying to cook on freezing mountain passes.

Camping Gaz can be obtained in Morocco and Tunisia as

---

1 Overland travel is full of contrasts, from the emptiness of the Tanezrouft Plateau in the Sahara to the congested streets of an Indian city such as Varanasi (formerly Banaras).

well as in some isolated parts of French-speaking Africa such as Dakar or Abidjan. Cylinders which fit Camping Gaz equipment can be hired from Ipragaz of Turkey, so if you are not going too far eastwards it might be worth using this brand.

Calor gas is widely used in homes, caravans and boats throughout the UK and gives good value for money. The refillable and exchangeable cylinders contain propane, which vaporises more readily than butane and is therefore more suitable for cold conditions. Calor cylinders are not exchangeable outside the British Isles and as they have a unique fitting are not easy to get refilled elsewhere. The main value of this brand is that the gas is cheap and available in cylinders that might be big enough to last a complete trip.

The author's experience is that 10lb of gas will run a two-burner stove cooking two meals a day for about three weeks, and a 32lb cylinder should last over two months when cooking fairly frequently for eight people. This big cylinder adds 64lb to the vehicle's load, however, and should ideally be carried externally or in a well-ventilated stowage.

If you run a motorised caravan with a gas-powered refrigerator and cooker, cylinder choice becomes a problem. If you are going far into Asia or Africa, it is best to use cylinders that can be refilled. Oil refineries (where cylinders are usually filled) are not supposed to fill cylinders from other countries in case they are not of a high enough specification to satisfy local regulations (cylinders for use in the tropics are generally designed to stand higher pressures resulting from the higher local temperatures). If a cylinder is overfilled, there is a risk of explosion. Different brands have different fittings, and unless the filling plant can match yours it will be impossible to get a refill.

A safe way of overcoming the problem is to use a cylinder

2 A useful trans-Africa outfit (*above*) a long wheelbase diesel Land-Rover with an ex-military trailer. Note the Dexion sand tracks on the roof rack, the steel tow rope and the roof rack mounting below the windscreen and the battery of roof-mounted cans. Lightweight tents can quickly be set up and dismantled (*centre*) and a shaded camp site is well worth finding in hot spots such as Ain Salah oasis (*below*).

with a safety valve. British Oxygen, which rents such cylinders to industrial users, may sell (possibly on a refund-on-return basis) a propane cylinder. The biggest are the most economical propositions, but overlanders with a vehicle of average dimensions will prefer the 25lb size or, for flexibility, two smaller cylinders. When one runs out, it can be refilled at leisure with the other as stand-by.

The author's experience may be useful here: using two 10lb cylinders, he ran a small refrigerator continuously and cooked most meals for two people for periods ranging from three to five weeks per cylinder. The cylinders were from Mobil, fitted with Kosangas bayonet fittings obtained in Zambia; they had safety valves and were capable of being refilled in Malawi, Kenya, India, Iran and Turkey.

It is possible, then, to carry enough gas for the round trip if sufficiently large cylinders can be loaded, but the problem remains of refilling from sources in other countries.

An easy way of overcoming this difficulty is to obtain from your supplier a bull-nose adaptor for your cylinder and extend it with a short length of gas pipe. Any LPG (liquefied petroleum gas) supply point can then clamp a flexible tube over the gas pipe to refill your cylinder, an operation which is well within the scope of small dealers decanting from a giant cylinder or supply tank.

Your original supplier should be able to sell you a bull-nose adaptor, gas pipe, hose, clips, and a suitable regulator.

Always use cylinders with a safety valve, which removes the danger of explosion from overfilling, and (ideally) mount them outside the vehicle but protect them from the direct rays of the sun.

Alternatives to gas

Petrol stoves are useful if you have a petrol-engined vehicle, but need to be treated with care and should not be used inside vehicle or tent as they can flare up unexpectedly. One of the most compact and efficient types is the Swedish Optimus, available with a twin burner. It may be worth taking a small petrol stove as a stand-by for gas.

Petrol is highly volatile in hot climates and the smallest spark can ignite the vapour and start a disastrous fire. It is best never to siphon it from the vehicle but to keep a small supply in a screw-cap metal can; a 1-litre oil can is ideal. Some American camping stoves need a refined white spirit which is difficult to get in most parts of the world.

Another traditional type of camping stove runs on paraffin (kerosene) and needs a small amount of methylated spirit (wood alcohol) or solid fuel pellets (Meta) to get it going. It is cheap, safer than a petrol stove, but sometimes temperamental and slow to start.

An emergency cooker can be made by half filling a large tin with loose dry sand and pouring half a pint of petrol into it. Hang a kettle over it from a tripod of tyre-levers or something similar and stand back when lighting it because the ignition is fierce.

Pots and pans

Nests of saucepans or billies are most compact and useful, and if you have enough space a pressure cooker is a worthwhile addition. Apart from its cooking function, it can be used as a sealed food container. It cooks food thoroughly at high altitudes, where water boils at lower temperatures. Space can be saved by fitting a nest of saucepans into a pressure cooker.

Keeping food or drinks cool

It is possible to buy small refrigerators designed for use in caravans and boats, and the most useful sort are powered by gas. The smallest sizes tend to be inefficient, but a capacity of about $1\frac{1}{2}$ cubic feet should be sufficient for a small party in the tropics. Those which are powered by the vehicle's electrical system are less practical because they cannot be left on for long when the engine is not running or they will flatten the battery.

If installing a gas refrigerator, follow the manufacturer's instructions and leave a hole under the unit to allow any leaking gas to escape. It is important to provide a vent pipe for the hot gases from the unit's burner.

Iceboxes and vacuum flasks have rarely proved useful on

overland trips. The former do not stay cool for long, become damp from condensation and begin to smell; the latter are effective but break easily. Both are bulky in relation to what they hold. The best way of keeping liquids cool is to use a container with an absorbent cover that can be kept moist. Government surplus aluminium water flasks wound with canvas webbing work well; an ordinary glass bottle can be wrapped in towelling bound with string or wire.

Canvas water bags are effective but usually leak until broken in.

PERSONAL GEAR

Bedding
A good sleeping bag is essential. Nylon and other synthetic materials are easiest to clean, fairly light and relatively cheap, and the most versatile are those that zip right down the side; they can be left open in hot climates. The mountaineers' and arctic explorers' cold-weather bags, besides being expensive, are generally too hot for overland use, but the bag you choose must be able to keep you warm.

A sheet sleeping bag, bought or home-made, will keep your less-easily-cleaned outer sleeping bag fresh for longer and in really hot places will provide light cover against draughts and insects if used on its own. A blanket is necessary if camping in winter conditions or at high altitudes. Locally hand-woven blankets make fine souvenirs and you could buy one during the trip. Alternatively, use a space blanket.

In humid tropical areas you will need a mosquito net, mosquito-proof tents, or (if sleeping in the vehicle) netting fitted to *all* open windows and ventilators. In less humid areas insect trouble can be avoided by careful choice of camping sites (not near stagnant water, marshy ground or maize cultivation) and the use of a good repellent. This does not remove the need to take anti-malaria precautions.

A good bed consists of a length of foam plastic $2\frac{1}{2}$in–3in thick which can be rolled up and carried in a canvas bag; it is light, cheap and unbreakable, and needs to be long enough to support head, trunk and hips only. Extra thickness is more valuable than length for comfort. A sweater or anorak makes a reasonable pillow. Airbeds are fine when new but tropical conditions and desert thorns cause them to deteriorate; a puncture outfit is essential, and a foot-pump useful.

The only camp bed that folds up small enough for most overland vehicles is a canvas stretcher supported on springy steel legs, which can damage groundsheets (and luggage if not carefully packed).

Hardy travellers could gouge a hollow in the ground sufficient for their hip and shoulder, but this is not advised for a person who is not used to this way of sleeping.

Eating equipment

This can be limited to a mug, a fairly deep plate, a knife, fork and spoon per person. Mugs and plates should be unbreakable plastic or metal, but handy camping cutlery and domestic cutlery are equally suitable.

Clothes and other necessities

Travellers should take no more than the minimum essential clothing, and a fair way to ration space is to issue a standard-size trunk or case to each member of the party and allow no more than that. There is always a tendency to take too much rather than too little.

It is impossible to say exactly what should be taken; the check-list given as an appendix will serve as a guide.

Valuables

A recommendation to bolt a metal box to the vehicle has already been made. If the vehicle is open or canvas-topped, a large metal cabin trunk can be used for additional security; some tour operators bolt steel chests to the roof racks of their vehicles.

You will need padlocks for all trunks and storage boxes, and for jerrycans and other equipment carried externally. Combination locks are acceptable provided a separate note is kept of the code. Make sure that the keyholes of external padlocks, particularly those at the rear, cannot get clogged with dust, and if necessary cover them with insulating tape.

Radios

The advantage of a radio is that it enables you to keep abreast of events in the world and particularly in countries further along your route (airmail editions of familiar newspapers, available in big towns, are usually several days out of date). Most transistor radios sold in western countries receive only on VHF (FM), medium and long wavebands but outside Europe the short wave ranges are needed. Medium and long wave and VHF pick up broadcasts from the country through which you are travelling, or its near neighbours, and it may be impossible to get distortion-free or audible reception from other sources. Select a radio which will receive on the short wavelengths, therefore, particularly the 19–49m bands, and which has fine tuning or a long tuning scale to facilitate location of distant stations.

FOOD, STORES AND GENERAL EQUIPMENT

Food

If your vehicle has the space or if you will be towing a trailer, take as much food as you can, to keep costs per head low. If you are restricted for space it is best to keep a stock of food sufficient for the occasions when no restaurant or shop is available or in case of breakdown miles from anywhere. It is always worth carrying a small supply of tea bags, instant coffee and perhaps packet soups or other light refreshments.

Protein is scarcest and most expensive almost everywhere, so stock up with a varied supply of meat and/or fish, either canned or freeze-dried, supplemented by freeze-dried peas and beans, which are light and compact. Flour-based foods and rice are generally available cheaply, but it is wise to start with some rice and perhaps spaghetti or noodles which can be replenished when necessary.

Potatoes are usually difficult or impossible to buy, and instant potato powder is an alternative, the main advantage being that it needs very little cooking and therefore saves fuel.

Beware of canned meat which is 90 per cent gravy; overlanders soon get bored with mushy stews or mince, and it is a good idea to vary the choice as much as possible with a selection of more solid meaty products such as braised steak, frankfurter sausages, hamburgers, chicken and corned beef. Take herrings, pilchards or tuna (canned sardines seem to be cheap and commonly available, even in remote stores and bazaars in the tropical jungle).

Tasty food is sold as pie filling—steak and kidney, chicken and mushroom and so on—and is better than meat pies which often consist largely of pastry or suet and need to be baked in an oven, which is wasteful of fuel.

Vesta freeze-dried meals are excellent overland cargo, being light and compact; the wrappings can be disposed of by burning. Some people are prejudiced against instant food, but the wide variety of different meals can be made more interesting by adding vegetables, packet soups, spices and so on.

Freeze-dried foods can be made more compact by throwing away the outer wrappings and repacking the inners in plastic picnic boxes.

There are two distinct types of packet soups, one taking about five minutes to cook and the other twenty. Taste difference is virtually nil, so choose the five-minute variety.

Extremely compact and nutritious foods are available from specialised camping stores which supply mountaineers and explorers. Though expensive, they are worth considering as emergency rations if you plan to travel light, such as on a motorcycle, or if you will be leaving your vehicle to explore on foot.

Canned cheese and butter improve the lunchtime slab of unleavened oriental bread, but are hard to find. Take the smallest tins; once opened, the contents must be used. Concentrated yeast extracts like Marmite are popular on bread in hot climates, as is soft cheese spread.

Bread of sorts can be obtained almost everywhere, except sometimes in remote Saharan oases or the smallest African villages. When none is available, a supply of rye bread or pumpernickel is a useful alternative. It is filling and is packed so thoroughly that it keeps well until opened. The compact brick-like pack loads easily.

Large 1½lb tins of instant coffee generally offer best value for money but smaller tins, which are probably cheaper in Britain than elsewhere, make acceptable presents in places where instant coffee is an expensive luxury.

Tea is best bought in tea bags. A cup of tea can be more refreshing than a cold drink in a hot climate.

Sugar, salt and similar necessities should be carried in secure plastic containers, clearly marked; paper or card packaging should never be relied on as it will chafe through.

Milk should be taken in powder form, but get the instant easy-to-mix type and not baby milk. A few small tins of condensed milk are worth considering but are heavy and, once opened, have to be used up. Powdered milk is rarely obtainable outside Europe and tends to be expensive, but condensed milk is universally available in small tins.

Jam and similar sticky substances should never be carried in glass jars; if not canned, they should be transferred to plastic containers. Beware of catering-size tins; jam softens in hot climates and its mass is sufficient to lift a plastic lid.

When buying food in quantity, avoid making economies by getting cheap or unknown brands or excessive quantities of a single 'bargain offer', which might turn out to be unpopular. If buying large quantities, approach a wholesale supplier; otherwise, practise haggling by trying to get the manager of your supermarket to give you a 'quantity discount'.

Although prices of mass-produced food might be higher outside Europe, it is not impossible to restock in parts of Africa and Asia and you need not feel obliged to carry enough food to last the trip. Even remote Kabul, capital of Afghanistan, has a couple of well-stocked supermarkets which are used mainly by the foreign and diplomatic community.

India has virtually no imported packaged foods, but produces good powdered milk, instant coffee and other packaged products. Bazaar and restaurant food is ultra-cheap and readily available. Africa is the continent where familiar food is not always easy to find, but the bigger towns and cities have adequate shops while cities like Kano, Lagos, Abidjan and Dakar in the west and Nairobi, Mombasa, Lusaka and Lubumbashi in the east have supermarkets stocked with most of the things you can buy at home, often reasonably priced.

A valuable food that can be bought anywhere, even in the remotest villages, is chicken eggs, and you should carry a plastic egg container capable of holding a dozen. Eggs are invariably safe to eat; yolks are often deeply coloured but unless the egg smells bad there is nothing to worry about. If you have no egg carrier, crack all the eggs into a sealable plastic container and have omelette or scrambled eggs later.

Be careful of local cheeses and other non-pasteurised dairy products as they carry fever and tuberculosis risk. Yoghurt is the exception, and as long as it appears clean and free from infection by flies is generally safe.

Housekeeping equipment

Every overland expedition needs a supply of the most concentrated washing-up liquid available. Used neat, it is effective for degreasing the mechanic's hands as well as washing clothes, apart from its normal purpose. Paper towels are much more effective than dishcloths, which soon become smelly and unhygienic. Paper towels have additional uses: mopping up spillages, wiping the engine dipstick and so on. J cloths, made from woven waterproof paper-fibre, are useful for washing up and can be thrown away when soiled or worn.

A large plastic bowl is essential for washing dishes, clothes, you and your fellow travellers, and it doubles as storage space for plates, mugs and cutlery. Additional cleaning equipment is a piece of foam plastic sponge and a small handbrush, essential for brushing dust and sand out of vehicle, tents and gear.

Toilet paper is not obtainable in many parts of the world except in western-orientated shops in large towns and cities. It can be used to supplement the supply of paper towels and is worth stocking up with, though one roll per person per week should be ample.

Do not forget clothes pegs and a length of washing-line.

FIRST AID AND MEDICAL EQUIPMENT

Each person should be responsible for individual medications, and this is particularly important for those who require regular medical treatment—they are in any case strongly advised to consult their doctor before embarking on an overland trip. For the party as a whole a good selection of first aid materials is required, plus a supply of drugs and medications sufficient to deal with the more common and simple health problems that can arise.

A biscuit tin makes a good container for the main first aid kit, but a supply of plasters, antiseptic and cotton wool should be accessible in a small container and everyone encouraged to use it when necessary. A small break in the skin, which at home might be ignored, easily becomes infected in dusty tropical environments.

The composition of the first aid kit depends on the nature of the expedition and the size of party; suggestions are given in an appendix. There is no point in taking elaborate surgical equipment unless a companion is medically qualified and able to use it. Ideally a member of the party should take a short course of training in first aid and should be responsible for organising the first aid kit and supervising its use on the journey (people should not help themselves from the main kit; the dashboard kit is for general use).

First aid is no substitute for qualified medical aid if doubt exists about a person's health.

General practitioners in the UK are not at liberty to prescribe quantities of drugs for use by people going abroad, but may be able to give useful advice.

Take sufficient anti-malaria pills to last the trip and follow the instructions carefully; some must be started two weeks before arrival in a malarial area (which includes Morocco if you are going to Africa) and must be continued for some time after you leave. Never change from one course to another or protection may be lost for a period. These points are important: malaria can be dangerous and even fatal. In some areas, particularly in the Far East, certain strains are resistant to some treatments, and the traveller should seek authoritative advice in good time.

Women should bear in mind that sanitary wear is difficult to obtain, and that an adequate supply should be kept in a damp-proof container.

MECHANIC'S DEPARTMENT: TOOLS AND SPARES

If heading into the Sahara and central Africa or off the beaten track anywhere else you should take at least one person who is a competent and experienced mechanic and who has a good idea of what tools and spares will be needed. His equipment will be among the heaviest in your load. His first task should be to obtain a full workshop manual for the vehicle and carry out a pre-departure check and overhaul, which should include the replacement of hoses, plugs, points, fan belt, filters, brake and clutch linings, rubbers in the hydraulic system, tyres, and so on, unless these parts are as good as new.

The mechanic's approach should be critical; he should anticipate trouble.

Nobody can be made into an instant mechanic as ability is based largely on experience, but keen amateurs could attend vehicle maintenance classes. The importance of being able to recognise and rectify vehicle faults cannot be overemphasised. If nothing were to go wrong in 10,000 miles it would be surprising, and failure to repair a small fault can lead to serious trouble later.

Basic equipment and tools

Specialised tools, spares and other equipment can be located in the UK in *Exchange & Mart*.

Before buying spanners, ascertain whether metric, AF (unified) or Whitworth are required for your vehicle and do not attempt to economise by settling for cheap tools.

The toolbox tends to get buried under other gear with the consequent danger that small adjustments and tightenings-up may be neglected. To guard against this, a kit of frequently needed light tools and wheel-changing equipment should be accessible, perhaps under a particular seat.

Spares and consumables

The mechanic must investigate what spares are likely to be needed, bearing in mind the condition of the vehicle and the nature of the journey. Most manufacturers or their distributors will advise if you ask for a list of recommended spares, and when contacting them you should give precise details of your vehicle including engine and chassis number. Land-Rover and Volkswagen are particularly helpful, both producing literature appropriate to the overlander, and the other large manufacturers are able to offer information on preparation of their vehicles and the scope of their overseas dealer network.

Even if you run an obsolete or ex-military vehicle it is still worth writing to the manufacturer.

The check-list in the appendix is a basic guide, though not exhaustive, and the prospective overlander will probably find it helpful to consider the vehicle's systems separately, as presented, when deciding on spares.

VEHICLE ACCESSORIES AND MODIFICATIONS

A sticker indicating the country of registration of the vehicle, not the nationality of the owner, is essential. Some countries, notably Germany, enforce the international law requiring cars to carry this. A reflective red warning triangle must be used when you stop on the open road in many countries, and Turkey demands two triangles, one 100 metres ahead of the vehicle and one 100 metres behind.

A fire extinguisher is a cheap insurance against what can be a frighteningly swift loss of the vehicle, especially if it is petrol-engined. If you are going to carry extra petrol or cook on petrol stoves, mount two big extinguishers in accessible positions.

A good tow rope is important; you may need it to tow or be towed. An engine temperature gauge and oil pressure gauge will give advance warning of faults which could, if neglected, lead to a seized-up engine—a sudden loss of engine oil or radiator coolant. Water-cooled engines may misfire when they overheat, due to escaping steam and water on the ignition leads, but this warning cannot be relied on and is absent in diesels and air-cooled engines. An oil temperature gauge can be fitted to an air-cooled engine. Drivers must develop the habit of glancing at gauges frequently because overheating can occur suddenly.

Extra fuel and water

This can be carried in cans or built-in tanks, but not in plastic containers, which are generally unsuitable for petrol (and illegal in some countries), taint water, and are liable to chafe. Metal jerrycans are best; some are coated internally to make them suitable for drinking water and are often available from ships' chandlers. A can that once held petrol or diesel fuel is extremely difficult to clean sufficiently for carrying drinking water.

Jerrycans can be strapped low down inside the vehicle and held with elastic luggage cords; better still, fix jerrycan holders to the outside. Do not carry cans of petrol on the front bumper because of the danger in a collision; diesel fuel is not inflammable enough to be a serious hazard. Cans carried on a roof rack put tremendous strain on the bodywork, so avoid carrying full cans on top except when absolutely essential, although from this position, the main fuel tank can be topped up by siphoning.

The most satisfactory arrangement is to build extra tanks, which can be made specially or adapted from old fuel tanks obtained from a breaker's yard. Land-Rovers and lorries usually have suitable underfloor spaces. A useful installation could allow for switching from one tank to another by the use of twin electric fuel pumps. Internal water tanks are best equipped with a manual or foot-operated suction pump. Lockable caps should be fitted to all filler pipes; this will prevent garage attendants from pumping the wrong liquid into the wrong compartment.

A major advantage of adding long-range tanks is that you can fill up with cheap fuel when approaching an expensive area.

Many countries charge duty on fuel in cans but never on fuel in tanks.

Air horns

These are strongly recommended; the horn fitted as standard to most vehicles is barely audible to the driver of a large vehicle such as a trans-Saharan truck roaring along in the middle of the *piste* in a cloud of dust. Cheap, reliable air horns such as the 2-trumpet Maserati are frequently on 'special offer' in vehicle accessory shops.

A powerful horn is needed in India where many lorries carry the slogan 'Horn please', and hooters have to be used so frequently that the electric type often burns out.

Guards

A sump guard provides good protection for the underside of the engine of low-slung vehicles. The sumps of Land-Rovers and similar vehicles are protected by the front axle, but if you are likely to drive through long grass which could hide termite hills and tree-stumps, a metal guard to protect the track rods is advisable. Guards can be obtained to prevent the propeller shaft universal joints from getting tangled with grass. Tall grass presents the hazard of a radiator clogged with seeds, which can be prevented by fitting gauze over the radiator grill; Land-Rover offer a 'chaff guard' as an optional extra. Many overlanders fit headlamp and windscreen guards made from stiff wire mesh, which is a security on gravelled roads.

If your vehicle has a large curved windscreen, it is worth investing in a plastic and wire emergency screen. Land-Rovers and other vehicles with flat windscreens are not so much at risk as flat laminated glass is widely available and can usually be cut to size.

Land-Rovers have big front ventilators which should be covered with gauze screens, bought as optional extras or home-made, and removable insect screens for night use over open windows should be made up from fibreglass mosquito netting fitted with Velcro fasteners.

Winches

Most 4-wheel-drive vehicles can be fitted with a winch designed as an optional accessory, driven mechanically or hydraulically off the engine, which means that it cannot be used when the engine cannot be run, for example in deep water or if the vehicle has turned on its side. In the author's opinion, the only useful powered winch for overland use is an electric one, which is cheaper than mechanical and hydraulic units and usually operates for a long period off the vehicle's battery, even in water or when the engine cannot be used.

Flexible and cheaper still, a lever-operated hand winch (a Crocodile hoist), normally used for construction work, pulls a length of $\frac{1}{4}$in cable with a load of up to five tons. Less-convenient alternatives are a chain block or rope block and tackle. All hand-operated devices can be used for purposes such as removing an engine or gearbox, but a winch or tackle is necessary only for ambitious multi-vehicle expeditions off the beaten track.

Sand tracks and chains

An aid for rescuing a vehicle axle-deep in sand or mud is essential for any 2-wheel-drive machine attempting a trans-African journey but is unnecessary on the main roads to the east.

Useful sand tracks that will carry a moderately heavy vehicle can be improvised from two 6ft lengths of Dexion 9in pressed steel plank, which is strong, fairly light, and can be bolted to the sides of the roof rack or strapped directly to the roof (with rubber padding to prevent damage to paintwork). Alternatively, a small engineering company could weld steel water pipe into two 4ft or 5ft ladders.

Wire mesh or even sacking makes a sand track for cars and light vehicles, and rope ladders have been effectively used for getting a light car through extensive sand.

Chains should be carried if you are likely to meet snow conditions, and are in any case compulsory in eastern Turkey in winter (end November–early March) even for 4-wheel-drive vehicles. Chains help a car through soft sand but are worn out in the process if used for long.

A shovel and small axe are invaluable, especially an ex-army entrenching tool which compactly combines both.

Insulation: heat, noise, dust

To make a double-skinned tropical roof, pop-rivet aluminium top-hat-shaped section channels to the existing roof as spacers and fit an aluminium sheet, cut to size beforehand, with rivets or self-tapping screws. Steel sheet bends more easily to a pronounced roof curve.

The simplest way of insulating the roof is to remove the lining trim and stick expanded polystyrene sheet to the metal, using the correct adhesive; the thinnest sheet is a good insulator against extremes of temperature and reduces condensation.

A lot can be done to reduce heat and noise by sticking felt inside the engine compartment, a worthwhile modification to noisy diesel vehicles. It is best to cover the engine bulkhead and the underside of the bonnet. Felt under the floor reduces transmission and tyre noise and keeps the floor cooler in hot climates. Use the correct automotive body felt, which is painted with fireproofing compound.

Dust, often as fine as talcum powder, will penetrate the smallest cracks and crevices. Most of it billows at the back of vehicles, so it is best to concentrate on curing bad seals around the rear windows, rear door or boot. A trailer keeps the dust from the back of the towing vehicle, but fills with dust itself. If it has a lid, foam rubber strips under the rim will help to seal it.

Some flat-backed vehicles benefit from a curved metal deflector fitted to the rear of the roof to create a down-draught

3 Be prepared for anything in the way of other road users. In Afghanistan passengers ride on the roofs of buses and lorries (*below left*) and lorries drive in the middle of the road—fine until two meet (*above left*). Much freight is hauled by slow-moving livestock such as the camel seen (*below right*) in Herat, Afghanistan or ox-carts in Andrah Pradesh, India (*above right*).

نفت گاز

which keeps the back window relatively clear of dust, spray or mud.

Improving fuel economy

The difference between adequate and accurate valve timing can be two or three miles to the gallon with a thirsty 4-wheel-drive vehicle. Valve timing adjustment is a major operation and should be carried out only by skilled mechanics following the manufacturer's instructions. It helps to overhaul the carburettor of a petrol engine and injectors of a diesel and to set sparking plug, contact breaker points and tappet clearances correctly. Heavy-footed driving wastes fuel, and a spring-loaded stop can be fitted to the accelerator linkage to restrict throttle opening; extra pressure must be used to override the device. A vacuum gauge, which indicates the correct level of acceleration, or an excess, encourages economical driving. Free-wheeling hubs are available for the front wheels of 4-wheel-drive vehicles but it is debatable whether they produce sufficient savings to justify their expense. Radial tyres kept at maximum pressures probably save more fuel than free-wheeling hubs. There is an overdrive unit for Land-Rovers which raises gear ratios by about 27 per cent, with consequent fuel saving, reduction of wear, increase of maximum speed and quietness level. An amateur mechanic can fit it.

Strengthening suspensions

A heavy load and rough roads increase the chance of suspension trouble. Many manufacturers offer optional heavy-duty suspensions, and if your vehicle is not fitted it is as well to

4   This fuel pump in Iran (*above*) measures petrol in litres and is calibrated 5, 10, 15, 20, etc up to 100 litres; the first numeral clockwise is 5, the last is 95. Each full revolution of the large hand measures 5 litres, so the dial in this photograph is reading 31 litres. Persian, as spoken in Iran, uses the same script as Arabic. Fuelling facilities may be primitive as in Ghanzi (*below*), a small town in the Kalahari in Botswana. The diesel fuel is hand-pumped direct from the drum and each glassful represents one gallon. Effective filters are essential.

change at least the rear springs and shock absorbers for the heavy-duty variety. Driving on rough roads with weak or worn-out shock absorbers will give an uncomfortable ride and reduced roadholding and throws a great strain on springs and shackles.

Land-Rover offer a reinforced front axle (standard on some models).

All manufacturers stress the need to avoid exceeding recommended maximum load. If you must carry more than the recommended weight, you should tow a trailer, get a bigger machine or take two vehicles.

Tyres

Radials are generally tougher than crossplies, have less rolling resistance (and therefore save fuel) and run cooler. Their initial cost is higher but they invariably more than save the difference in cost by lasting much longer. Tubeless tyres are inadvisable because impact with stones and potholes can cause sudden deflation and it is not usually possible to reinflate the tyre without a high-pressure air supply.

Heavy tread patterns have an advantage in sand and mud but not enough to outweigh their extra expense and disadvantages under ordinary road conditions. Sand tyre treads pick up nails and bits of stone and metal more readily than road tyres, are noisy on hard roads, heat up and so wear out sooner. This criticism applies to track grips, tyres with treads like those on tractor rear wheels, which have the added disadvantage of being hazardous on wet or icy hard road surfaces. It is worth fitting the largest tyre section your wheels can take, especially if you intend running on soft ground. Large tyres give more protection against getting bogged down than a cog-like tread, and also improve the vehicle's ground clearance.

It is easy to forget inner tubes when fitting new tyres. A lot of tyre trouble is caused by perished and porous inner tubes, and a new set is quite cheap when compared with the cost of the outer casings.

GETTING THE VEHICLE READY

Mechanical parts

The mechanic's pre-departure check and overhaul should leave nothing to chance. Repairs during the journey may be troublesome and expensive, and a job that is quite simple at home can be hell when it is 110 degrees in the shade. Where a particular model of vehicle is known to have a mechanical weakness, the parts should be renewed; anyone running a Land-Rover IIa should change both rear half shafts for new ones before departure (a half-hour job) and take the old ones as spares. Replacing them once broken, a fairly common problem with this model, can take several hours. Volkswagen owners could raise the rear suspension and replace the torsion bars and shock absorbers. All users of petrol-engined vehicles should investigate retarding the ignition to cope with lower octane fuel.

Check the compression and oil pressure of an elderly engine and if necessary have it rebored and fit new bearings, at the same time changing the oil seals and decoking and overhauling the cylinder head and valve assembly.

Investigate the gearbox and transmission and change worn items. Complete exchange engines and transmissions are often advertised in *Exchange & Mart*.

Repair or replace corroded parts of the chassis or underside. Check and replace if necessary all springs and shock absorbers, in any case renewing the rubber shock absorber mounting bushes.

Tighten all nuts and bolts under the vehicle and check nuts locked with split pins; nuts that stay tightly done up on tarred roads will loosen on corrugated dirt roads. Wire insecure cables in place, paying attention to the handbrake cable on Ford Transits, which can drop on to the prop shaft.

Fit dust covers to mechanical joints under the vehicle. You can protect the front prop shaft of Land-Rovers by fitting a rubber sleeve of the sort normally fitted only to the rear shaft. Volkswagen recommend fitting a felt seal between the steering column and its outer tube to prevent stiffness caused by dust.

If you plan to tow a trailer, check the chassis structure around the towing hitch, an area which is vulnerable to corrosion and even when in good condition can be too weak to cope with the severe jerks and impacts resulting from towing a heavy trailer fast across soft and uneven ground. The author modified his Land-Rover by having substantial steel reinforcing plates welded to the rear of the chassis and the cross-member that carries the towing hook. Other weak points are where the chassis carries the spring and shock absorber mountings; these may benefit from reinforcement if your vehicle is elderly or heavily loaded. Such modifications are less critical on trips that will follow tarred or well-maintained gravel roads. Welding is expensive, but it is always much cheaper to have a weak point reinforced than to have repairs done after it has broken.

Electrical items have a reputation for being troublesome, so fit an exchange starter motor, generator and a new battery if the existing ones are suspect.

It is worth fitting right-hand-dip bulbs if you plan to drive at night in right-hand-drive countries, but yellow headlights are not necessary even in France, where the curious national law is not imposed on foreigners. Yellow headlights lack power and if badly adjusted are no less dazzling to oncoming drivers than badly adjusted white ones. It is better to adjust white lights correctly than to paint them yellow.

Roof rack or trailer?

The most popular method of carrying extra luggage is a roof rack, which allows light, bulky items to be carried conveniently. It also encourages overloading, raises the vehicle's centre of gravity causing it to lean more than usual on corners, and increases wind resistance and therefore fuel consumption. Luggage on roof racks is vulnerable to theft, rain, dust and damage by branches of trees, and the weight can damage the roof and body of the vehicle.

A roof rack for an overland trip should be strongly constructed from welded steel tubes, not made of lightweight metal or pressed steel. It will not be cheap. A roof rack for a Land-Rover should have extended legs at the front to transfer some weight either to the windscreen mounting lugs on the front bulkhead or, with a full-length rack, through legs to the front bumper; the front part of a Land-Rover's roof is supported only by the windscreen frame and is not capable of carrying a substantial load.

The only trailers really suitable for arduous conditions are ex-military trailers designed for towing behind a Land-Rover or jeep. Light commercially produced trailers are far too flimsy. All-metal ex-army trailers with large wheels and effective brakes can often be bought cheaply at auctions; the best type is designed to carry half a ton at speed over rough ground but is light enough when empty for one person to wheel. Heavy luggage can go in the trailer, saving the towing vehicle's suspension from wear. It offers no noticeable wind resistance and has a negligible effect on cornering ability. However, there is extra expense in shipping, particularly across the English Channel, and reversing becomes a skilled art.

You can tow a trailer across the Sahara only if you have a 4-wheel-drive machine to pull it, and Algerian regulations stipulate that it should not exceed one-third of the weight of the towing vehicle when loaded, which is sensible. Towing a caravan is not practical on any overland route and illegal on the trans-African one.

An ex-army trailer is best covered with a home-made lid of aluminium sheet to prevent theft and keep the contents dry and dust-free. This is a straightforward job for a handyman, who should at the same time be able to rig up a means of padlocking the lid.

A number of long-haul overland operators use ex-army trailers behind Bedford RLs and Land-Rovers on the trans-African routes.

Make sure that your insurance is amended to allow for towing a trailer; a small extra premium may be payable.

Specialist help with vehicle preparation

Many of the suggested modifications may be difficult for anyone lacking elaborate workshop facilities. Several small firms specialise in making up special fittings, supplying spares and equipping expedition vehicles—work which most general garages would shun or charge heavily for.

PACKING AND LOADING

When packing, put things you need frequently where you can get at them; pack carefully to prevent your load moving around and getting damaged or rattling. Other considerations are to protect your equipment from dust, the weather and theft.

If it is not possible to build shelves and cupboards into the vehicle, boxes of wood, tin, or even tough cardboard can be used. If the containers are marked A, B, C, etc, and items within each container also marked, a manifest can then be prepared; for example, 'C5 Fuses' would mean that packet 5 in box C contains fuses. As consumable items are used they can be struck off the list, giving a clear idea of the need for restocking. If this seems like too much trouble, simply list the contents with a felt-tipped marker on each box.

Heavy items like canned food, tools and spare parts should be packed low down and near the front with nothing squashable in front of or underneath them. A good way of securing things and preventing rattles is to strap the load in place with hooked elastic cords, and wedge offcuts of foam plastic between hard items that might rattle or damage each other. The only safe way of carrying glass or china crockery is to store it in carefully designed cupboards fitted with clips or securing loops for each item.

Large spares can be stowed externally in nooks and crannies under the vehicle, and Land-Rovers sometimes carry spare springs secured to the front bumper with shackle pins. Spares such as ignition coils and electric fuel pumps can be bolted alongside the existing parts so that they will be ready for immediate use if needed. Tow rope, lengths of hose, electric cable, jump leads, fan belts and other flexible items can be coiled and stored in the centre of the spare wheel (which would need a well-secured cover if carried externally). Most cross-country vehicles have space under the floor for a toolbox. Long parts like half shafts and torsion bars can often be carried across the top of chassis members, but be careful that they cannot crush a fuel or brake line. If spares are carried underneath, it is best not to rely on wire alone to hold them in place; make brackets of steel strip and bolt them directly to a strong base. Dexion slotted angle or punched strip is a convenient material for brackets.

Avoid loading heavy items on a roof rack. You will need a tarpaulin to hold the load in place and keep the rain off, and the most successful material is probably heavy-gauge PVC sheeting with reinforced brass eyelets. Light canvas and other woven materials shred quickly once a small tear starts and heavy canvas is expensive and bulky. Take a lot of elastic cords for holding the roof rack cover; tropical sun soon perishes rubber and many will snap during the journey.

The same loading principles apply to a trailer as to the towing vehicle. It is worth balancing a trailer to keep minimum weight on the towing hitch; not only does this take strain off the rear of the towing vehicle, but the trailer will handle better under way and when being manhandled. It is wise to provide a solid barrier of some sort to keep heavy objects from moving forward under the suspension's bouncing influence.

On the Road

DRIVERS AND DRIVING

Who should drive?
One person, preferably mechanically minded, should take complete charge of driving and vehicle maintenance and decide who drives and when. All drivers should be named on insurance documents, and premiums will generally be higher if the list includes a person with a bad driving record, a person under 21, or someone who has driven for a short time only. A tactful way of keeping reckless or inexperienced drivers away from the wheel is to leave them off the insurance proposal form in the first place. The highest risk involved in an overland trip is that of having an accident caused by bad driving, and a cautious and experienced driver not only reduces the risk of accidents but also of expensive breakdowns, through his or her sensitivity to variations in the vehicle's behaviour.

The driver of the moment should take full responsibility for refuelling, checking oil, water, tyre pressures, and the general condition of the vehicle. Back seat driving is best discouraged from the start.

Intending drivers should if possible practise for a couple of hours on a skid pan; the AA, RAC or local authority should know where the nearest one is.

If a trailer is to be towed, reversing practice is suggested.

Remember that the person who has spent the day driving or working on the vehicle does not wash up after supper.

Driving hazards

Driving standards vary enormously and drivers are generally much less disciplined outside western Europe. Overland drivers must never assume anything about other road users except that they are unpredictable. Lorries pull out of side roads without warning, few drivers seem to use rear-view mirrors, buses and taxis overtake, catch a glimpse of a potential passenger, and swerve across your path to stop. Pedestrians in rural areas lack traffic sense and might run across the road in front of a vehicle they have not heard or seen, or because they have totally misjudged its speed. Be particularly careful of pedestrians running out from behind parked lorries or buses.

Driving in Asian cities can be nerve-racking; Tehran, Beirut and Bangkok must in the author's experience be tackled with care and calmness, and a watch must be kept at traffic lights for drivers who cannot be relied on to stop at red. Taxis usually follow fixed routes and weave in and out of traffic in their search for passengers. The pace in Indian cities is slower, with livestock wandering in the main streets, but drivers should take care on the dual carriageway into Delhi from the south; vehicles travel in both directions on each carriageway and unpredictably criss-cross through gaps in the central reservation.

African cities tend to be more modern, having grown up in the motor age, and have broad boulevards. Traffic is light but this leads to a lack of discipline. While Asian drivers are rarely drunk, since alcohol is prohibited by their religions, the overlander in Africa should keep his eye open for erratic driving, especially in the evenings and on Sundays.

This need not alarm the driver who is careful, unhurried, and able to anticipate potential danger. The horn should be used at all danger spots.

Night driving

Of the many overlanders the author has met, he knows few who have been involved in accidents and only one case where there were serious injuries. Almost without exception, the accidents happened at night.

Great Britain and other countries with heavy traffic have developed high standards of road discipline and maintenance. You would not expect to find unlit roadworks or blatantly dangerous night parking, but although they are not common such things do occur in countries where traffic is light. Unlit ox-carts are a serious night-time hazard.

Some drivers do not dip headlights at all; others switch them off completely and drive on sidelights, occasionally flashing to main beam to see what is ahead (Greek drivers are fond of this technique). Many vehicles are badly maintained and may show no rear lights, but patriotic Iranian lorry drivers may use dozens of coloured lights in their national colours, which makes it difficult to judge whether the red, white and green Christmas tree seen in the distance is coming or going. The rule of red lights to the rear and white to the front is only approximate in some parts of the world, and vigilance must be increased accordingly.

Common night-time hazards in remote areas are narrow bridges, rocks left in the road by lorry drivers who use them to prevent their stationary vehicles from rolling, or rocks that have rolled down hillsides. Chasms can form in the road surface after heavy rain and small bridges are swept away. None of these would present much risk in daylight but all can be very dangerous at night, when it is essential to be able to stop within the range of visibility. Stop if badly dazzled by oncoming traffic.

Animals can cause problems at night. One of the worst is the kudu, a magnificent antelope with long corkscrew horns, which attempts to jump over headlight beams. Kudu run very fast, and as fully grown males can weigh 600lb a collision can be devastating. Driving at night is not normally allowed in game reserves, but care should be taken in the few other kudu areas of central and southern Africa. At the other end of the speed spectrum, the black Indian water buffalo will amble straight into the beams of your headlights. If you stop, he will walk up to the front of your vehicle and stand there, sometimes with a cart and sleeping driver, until you switch your lights out or drive round him.

Choosing a camp site in the dark is not easy, and another disadvantage of night driving is that points of interest are missed. Because of the dangers and drawbacks, driving during the hours of darkness is best avoided.

Animal psychology

Away from areas with heavy motor traffic there will be more and more livestock on the road, and you will find that different species have distinct reactions to vehicles. Cows, and particularly calves, are so unpredictable that it is essential to slow right down whenever one is met near the road. Sheep are more predictable as they will usually move in one direction, following their leader. Goats react to a toot on the horn by scurrying to safety. Horses are prone to panic if hooted at but donkeys and mules rarely panic and a loud blast is often the only way to make them move aside. Camels will slouch out of the way, but allow for the possibility that their legs may be hobbled together. Chickens scatter in all directions, and may double back on their tracks.

There are, unfortunately, only limited areas in the world where wild animals may be seen, but in such areas they can be a hazard. Giraffes are as unpredictable as cows, but faster, better camouflaged and very much bigger. The African buffalo is one of the few animals who might charge; he is more than a match for all except a lorry. Never drive near animals with young, particularly elephants, which can be violent if offspring are thought to be in danger. Elephants demonstrate their anger by spreading their ears, trumpeting and raising their trunks, and when these signs are seen it is best to drive off quickly; elephants can run at 30mph and are much nimbler than they look. Rhinos, which are rare, are less dangerous than they appear and may even miss if they charge.

Most wild animals in game reserves have become accustomed to motor vehicles and may seem almost tame—but they are not. Getting out of a vehicle to wander around is not only unwise but a serious offence in many game parks, and harassing creatures by hooting or driving too close is cruel apart from being illegal. They are more likely to attack if they feel threatened. Wherever they are encountered, wild animals should be treated with respect and disturbed as little as possible.

ROADS AND TRACKS

Maintained dirt roads

Most untarred through-routes are regularly maintained but in spite of this may be bone-shatteringly rough at times. The best surfaces to be expected are of freshly graded gravel, mud or laterite. Grading is carried out by a large earth-moving machine with an angled scraper which planes off the rough top surface and spews it out along the side of the road or sometimes down the middle. Every so often new material is dumped on the road and rolled into the surface to replace material previously graded off. Piles of material are occasional obstacles.

A newly graded smooth surface with well-banked curves allows high cruising speeds but loose, dry gravel and coarse sand can cause a slide or skid. In wet conditions the reverse is true: wet gravel is no more slippery than dry, but wet, smooth mud or laterite can be like ice.

Driving fast and safely on dirt roads depends on an instinctive feel for the handling of the vehicle on different surfaces, an ability which comes only with experience. After driving a lot on untarred roads the driver will begin to develop a knack of reading the road surface and sensing the danger spots, but until this can be done reliably it is best to drive slowly, particularly on mountain tracks or roads with deep ditches on either side. A skid in those situations could be disastrous.

Dust

Untarred roads are always dusty when dry. Lorries and buses trail thick clouds which, if there is little or no wind, billow out for hundreds of yards behind. This provides a strong incentive to overtake as quickly as possible, but reduced visibility makes it difficult and dangerous. Use main beam headlights when entering the dust cloud and sound the horn in continuous blasts as soon as you are close behind the vehicle you want to pass. The driver probably cannot see you in his mirror so make sure he knows you are there before overtaking, in case he swerves to dodge a pothole or overtake something.

A dust cloud usually drifts to one side of the road and it is possible to drive on the clearer side to see the road ahead.

Corrugated surfaces

The rhythmic bouncing of motor vehicle wheels on spring-loaded suspensions beats a series of regular indentations into untarred road surfaces. These grow cumulatively worse and, if the road is not regraded, a corrugated surface appears with bumps and dips quite evenly spaced every two or three feet. Their severity is greatest on the approaches to curves and at other points where traffic has to brake. If the corrugations are not too severe, it is possible and preferable to drive fast because the wheels touch the high spots and skip across the valleys; at slower speeds, the wheels follow the contours of the road surface. Thus at 40–50mph a smoother and less-damaging ride than at 15–20mph is possible.

A vehicle's wheels are airborne for some of the time when travelling fast over corrugations, and as their grip on the road surface is correspondingly reduced there is an increased risk of skidding. More care than usual is needed to anticipate hazards as it is not possible to stop so readily. Care must also be taken when driving on steeply cambered corrugated surfaces as the reduced grip of the tyres may allow a sideways slide. Many loose-surfaced roads are deliberately given a high camber to help rain water run off, and it is best to drive with the wheels straddling the peak of the camber when you are going fast, and where visibility is good enough to allow it.

Corrugations can be so severe that it is impossible to overcome them with speed. This is because the bulk of traffic in many areas is large lorries which form ridges deep enough to swallow the smaller wheels of a car. The smaller the wheels of the vehicle, the more sensitive it will be to corrugations, and in such situations there is no alternative but to travel at the maximum speed you and your vehicle can bear, probably no more than 15mph. Heavy trucks in some areas usually drive down the middle of the road, and it may be possible to avoid the irregularities by driving at the edge.

Other rough surfaces

Impacted stony surfaces have bumps randomly distributed, and cautious driving is required. Tough cross-country machines are capable of taking a certain amount of battering from uneven roads but softer-sprung vehicles like minibuses and cars should be driven slowly to avoid damage. The bigger the wheels, the less effect bumps will have.

Always keep a watchful eye on the road ahead for loose stones or rocks, which sometimes become uprooted and will ruin a tyre or damage suspension if hit at speed. Vehicles with twin rear wheels can pick up loose rocks between the tyres, which will soon wreck sidewalls, so check the rear wheels at every stop after driving on stony roads.

In desert areas with little surface sand or soil cover, tracks are sometimes graded across outcrops of shale, limestone or slate-like rock strata which are brittle and sharp-edged. It is wise to drive very slowly here, with tyres blown up hard, perhaps 10–20 per cent over the recommended pressures, as this makes treads less likely to pick up fragments of sharp stone.

Corrugations form channels for rainwater and heavy rains may leave accentuated gullies across a road, especially on the steeper cambers found on curves. These can be so deep that they make the road impassable and could wreck a vehicle driving into them at speed. Such road damage is usually quickly repaired, but often in a makeshift way with large rocks or pieces of timber, so after heavy rain watch out for washouts as well as crude road repairs.

Fording water

The depth of water that can be forded depends not only on the type of vehicle but also on how it is driven. A carelessly handled Land-Rover can be swamped in water shallow enough to allow the passage of a carefully driven Mini. With a petrol-engined vehicle, the limiting factor is the depth of water needed to reach the ignition leads or distributor; once the ignition system is swamped the engine will stall. This normally happens in shallower water than the depth needed to swamp the ignition if the car were standing still, because the forward movement throws up a bow wave which pours back through the radiator and is sprayed all over the engine by the cooling fan. The faster you drive through water, the higher the bow wave and the sooner your ignition will be swamped, so the sensible course is to go as slowly as possible.

Stop before entering the water, engage first gear or low ratio, and keeping the engine speed as high as possible crawl through the flood. Slipping the clutch can help to keep the engine speed up and avoid the risk of stalling if you hit a submerged obstacle. It is not serious if the exhaust pipe becomes submerged because the exhaust gases have sufficient pressure to bubble out provided you keep the engine revving, but if you stall in deep water the silencer might fill and make restarting difficult.

If you stall, first try restarting as the ignition often gets swamped by spray and will dry out in a few minutes from the heat of the engine. If all else fails, the vehicle can be moved a few yards in first or reverse gear by driving it with the starter motor, first unloading passengers (who can push) and heavy items. To reduce resistance still further, remove the sparking plugs but take care that water does not get into the cylinders.

To ford deeper water a number of extra precautions can be taken, the first being to waterproof the ignition. The easiest way is to use water-repellent aerosol spray, but Vaseline is an effective substitute if liberally smeared over the ignition leads and distributor cap. Grease will do, but most lubricating greases attack rubber and should be carefully cleaned off all rubber insulation afterwards. A polythene bag can be tied over the distributor.

The fan belt can be removed and cardboard placed across the front of the radiator in order to reduce the amount of water entering the engine compartment and to prevent any that does from being thrown all over the engine by the fan.

Disconnecting the fan makes the ignition light come on because the generator is normally driven by the fan belt, and it will also make the engine overheat, so run the engine for short periods only in this state and watch the water temperature gauge. Jeeps have a handle beside the generator which allows instant slackening of the fan belt.

If the ignition is well waterproofed, or if you have a diesel-engined machine which has no ignition system, the next sensitive part to protect is the air intake. It is vital to prevent water entering. Land-Rovers and similar cross-country vehicles have an optional extension for fitting to the air intake, and in an emergency a Land-Rover air cleaner can be raised on its flexible tube fixing and fastened or held at a safe height. Many minibuses and cars have air cleaners bolted directly over the carburettor, usually with the intake pipe pointing forward. These are particularly vulnerable to being swamped but can often be protected by fitting a spare radiator hose over the intake tube and curving it so that its open end faces backwards; care must be taken to avoid making a kink which will choke the engine, and to fasten the temporary extension firmly. A hose clip will hold it.

If you plan to drive through deep water frequently, it is advisable to take precautions to stop water entering mechanical parts by blocking breather holes on axles, gearbox and clutch housing. Land-Rovers have a plug for screwing into the clutch housing drain hole.

Once the weight is off the wheels a vehicle is liable to be washed away, something which can be avoided by opening a door and flooding the interior. It will not usually be necessary with cross-country vehicles, which are heavy and fairly leaky, but Volkswagens will float in surprisingly shallow water.

There is always a danger of hitting submerged obstructions, deep mud, quicksand or potholes, and all floods and fords should first be investigated on foot; they may look three inches deep but have a two-foot-deep washout in the middle (*see Plate 5*). It is best to paddle through, testing the depth and making a mental note of the best path to take. Watch out for heavy pieces of timber laid lengthwise along the ruts by lorry drivers debogging their lorries; a small vehicle can cause one end to see-saw up and jam under its chassis.

There is a lot of danger from fast-running water, and a person doing reconnaissance on foot should be secured by a rope around the waist, kept taut.

Stagnant or slow-moving river water in most parts of tropical Africa may be infected with the bilharzia parasite, and if you have to wade into this kind of water you should arrange a medical test for bilharzia after you complete your journey.

Water too deep to drive through

If the water is not fast-flowing or impossibly deep, unload completely, block all breathers and filler points with self-adhesive waterproof tape, polythene or other suitable materials and get a lorry to pull you through. You will often be expected to pay for this kind of help and should negotiate a price in advance to prevent ill-feeling afterwards. If you have two vehicles, you can use one to pull the other through by fitting up a suitably secured pulley block on the far bank provided that you have sufficient rope to span the water twice. Never drive a second vehicle into water until the first is safely through, even if the water does not appear deep.

A hand winch should pull a vehicle through any depth of water if a suitable anchor point is available on the far bank; in the absence of a large rock or tree stump, bury the spare wheel a foot or so below the surface to provide an effective anchor. If you have no equipment, you may need to hire local villagers; thirty men or a couple of oxen can move the average overland vehicle across most obstacles. Negotiate a price in advance.

After the crossing

Your brakes will be wet enough to make them useless until dried, so test them immediately and if necessary drive with your foot on the pedal until they bite again and pull evenly. Never fail to do this.

Change the engine oil as soon as possible; if water has entered the sump, it will raise the oil level (oil floats on water), to an extent which jeopardises proper lubrication. Oil affected by water goes creamy.

Driving on soft surfaces

On soft surfaces, wheels sink into the ground, and must constantly be attempting to climb out of their own ruts. The deeper the wheels sink, the greater the resistance, until finally the driven wheels spin uselessly and the vehicle bogs down.

Get into the correct gear before hitting a soft patch; do not change gear on the way through unless absolutely unavoidable. Four-wheel-drive vehicles have a great advantage over other machines in that wheelspin happens less easily; the situation is aggravated for most vehicles because the differential gears allow one wheel to spin while the other stands still. This turns 2-wheel drive into 1-wheel drive, and 4-wheel drive into 3- or 2-wheel drive. Keep driving actions as smooth and careful as possible; watch the surface ahead and constantly plan the route by visualising the path you wish the wheels to follow. If conditions look particularly difficult or you are uncertain of what lies ahead, stop and explore on foot.

When picking your route, bear in mind:

> The momentum of a fast-moving vehicle will help to overcome drag and reduce the traction needed, so it is best to find a route that is clear of obstacles and level enough to be taken at speed.
>
> Remember the action of the differential gears and choose a path that maintains similar conditions under both wheels of each axle.
>
> For the same reason, take care on uneven ground to find a course that will prevent wheels being lifted clear of the ground or cause excess weight to be thrown on one wheel.
>
> Pick a route that will not ground the vehicle.
>
> The best indication of ground softness is the depth of ruts left by other vehicles. Compare the appearance of the surface with other areas known to have been soft; sand drifts often look different from firmer ground and experience will show that dark discolorations commonly cover fine, soft white sand known as *fesh-fesh* which can bog a vehicle in a few yards.

Once you have decided on the best path, engage a suitable gear, probably second, and drive as fast as reasonable and safe through the soft patch.

Problems with sand

When driving on hard-surfaced tracks through sandy country, be careful of small drifts of windblown sand. These sometimes compact into rock-hard ridges a few inches high which can be damaging if hit at speed. Softer patches of sand may snatch the steering out of your hands.

Sandstorms are a menace; some last only a short time, others blow for weeks. The area between El Goléa and Ain Salah in the Sahara often has a short sandstorm in the late afternoon which stops quite suddenly once the sun sets, but the 'wind of a hundred days' blows out of central Asia and across the main road into Afghanistan, hurling dust and grit through every gap in the Parapamisus Hills for three months of the year. If caught in a short, violent sandstorm, drive well clear of the road and stop with the front of the vehicle facing away from the wind to prevent too much sand blowing into the engine. If possible, take shelter behind a rock outcrop or a hill. In less severe or more permanent storms, use headlights on full beam to warn oncoming traffic and close all windows and ventilators (you can sometimes open those on the leeward side). After covering any distance in such conditions, check the air cleaner and change oil and filter if necessary.

Certain sandy regions such as the Tanezrouft plateau in the Sahara have surfaces that are not soft enough to stop a vehicle but greatly increase drag and impose conditions similar to driving hundreds of miles continuously uphill, causing a great increase in fuel consumption (often 50 per cent more than normal). This must be allowed for when stocking up with fuel. As these regions are generally very hot, vehicles are likely to overheat and a regular watch should be kept on the engine temperature gauge. The only way to keep the temperature down is to engage a lower gear, thus increasing engine speed and spinning the cooling fan faster. Water circulation can be improved by removing the thermostat and blocking any thermostat bypass.

The Tanezrouft and similar areas are firmer to drive on in the early morning and at night as cooler conditions cause the surface to consolidate slightly, while heat expands air between the surface sand grains and loosens them, so it is worth setting off just before daylight and stopping during the hottest part of the day.

Severe drag from sand is experienced when driving in the sandy thorn-bush country on the southern fringes of the Sahara, in Niger, Mali, Chad and the Sudan and in most of the Kalahari Desert. In these areas, dense bush forces all vehicles to follow the same narrow track which soon develops two deep ruts full of loose sand, offering so much resistance that Land-Rovers frequently need second gear for stretches of many miles at a time, which can more than double fuel consumption.

Slippery conditions

Chains provide useful extra grip in mud and snow, which should be tackled at a steady and carefully controlled speed. If there are other vehicle tracks, keep in them and avoid turning the front wheels more than necessary. Explore difficult stretches on foot first. If stopped by a snowdrift you can often break through by driving at it again and again, or, if you have 4-wheel drive or front-wheel drive, by spinning the wheels while winding the steering from side to side to saw away at the drift sufficiently to get going again.

Melting snow is the most slippery of all; once the temperature has fallen well below freezing, driving is easier and safer.

Debogging techniques

When a vehicle sticks with its wheels deep in soft ground, never try moving it by spinning the wheels or it will, within seconds, be up to its axles. First try reversing out, using the clutch very gently and declutching immediately if the wheels spin. All passengers should get out and push, preferably by crouching with their backs against the vehicle, legs slightly bent, and straightening their legs while pushing their heels into the ground. This uses strong leg muscles for most of the push and gives a better grip on the ground than when pushing in the conventional forward-facing way. By holding the underside of the bumper or the body of the vehicle while lifting, the pushers transfer some of the vehicle's weight off its wheels and on to their feet (*Fig 1*).

Fig 1 *Simultaneous pushing, lifting and bouncing*

If this also fails, the sand will have to be cleared away from the wheels. If brushwood or stones are available, push them under the tyres and repeat the attempt. Alternatively, rock the vehicle by changing rapidly from first gear to reverse without allowing the wheels to spin. Fast fore-and-aft rocking will often free a trapped vehicle, particularly if the passengers push in unison (they must be ready to jump if it breaks free suddenly).

If all these methods fail, sand tracks should be used and the vehicle kept moving until clear of the soft patch. To avoid having to walk back a long way to retrieve the sand tracks, tie them to the back of the vehicle. Sacking, chicken wire, and even rubber floor-mats (which will probably get ruined) can be used, and reducing tyre pressures to perhaps 10lb/sq in or less gives noticeable extra traction on soft ground but will cause serious damage if the tyres are not blown up again soon after. Pumping in hot conditions is arduous and the method is a last resort.

A winch or chain block can be used to pull the machine through the worst stretches; a small item like a length of steel pipe will hold the cable if it is buried three or four feet deep at right angles to the direction of pull.

Where attempts to shift the vehicle have met with failure, the wheels could be raised one at a time with the jack or suitable levers and a firmer surface built under them with sticks, stones and branches. If nothing solid can be found, it is often sufficient to fill in the tracks with sand or mud and reverse the unloaded vehicle out with lowered tyre pressures and all passengers pushing.

If the vehicle is bogged in deep mud or mud submerged under water, it may not be possible to use a jack. Fortunately, timber is usually available in wet situations. Push one or two substantial poles or logs lengthways under the vehicle and use another as a lever to lift the vehicle, pivoting against a strong part of the chassis and one of the recumbent poles (*Fig 2*).

Fig 2 Raising a vehicle with logs as support

Aim to lift one corner of the vehicle and one wheel at a time while someone pushes solid material underneath. When all four wheels have been raised, fill the wheel ruts to facilitate exit.

The spare wheel can be used beneath the vehicle as a rest for a lever (*Fig 3*).

Cross-country driving

When driving off the main route to look for a camp site or explore game reserves, you might cross ground that has never been used as a track. Some tracks are themselves so bad that they resemble unbroken terrain. Driving in such conditions should be attempted only in suitable vehicles and parties should never wander far from a recognisable track in remote areas without an experienced guide and at least two vehicles, because help will not be forthcoming in case of breakdown or if you are lost.

Fig 3   Raising a vehicle with spare wheel as support

When descending a steep slope with a loose or soft surface, use the gears (not the brakes) to slow the vehicle. Four-wheel-drive vehicles should use low ratio so that the vehicle crawls down the slope on the overrun. Braking can cause a slide which may turn the vehicle over if it swings around at right angles to the slope. For this reason tackle all steep slopes directly, even though this is the steepest approach, as a vertical vehicle position is the most stable and assists traction. If you stall when climbing steeply and are unable to restart, roll backwards to the bottom with lowest reverse gear engaged; never attempt to turn as this could cause you to roll over.

Care must be taken that the vehicle's rear overhang does not ground at the foot of a sudden incline, such as when leaving a dried-up watercourse or starting to climb an embankment.

Use of 4-wheel drive

Apart from its use in obvious situations such as fording rivers or crossing soft ground, 4-wheel drive improves roadholding, braking and traction in slippery conditions such as those found on many tarred roads in hot countries, which develop a smooth, almost glazed surface which after a shower of rain becomes as treacherous as black ice. This is a great danger to unsuspecting motorists when they first reach Mediterranean and tropical countries.

Four-wheel drive increases fuel consumption. It should not be used on hard non-slippery surfaces as there is normally no differential gearing between front and rear axles; this results in tyre and transmission wear.

A 4-wheel-drive vehicle with low ratio engaged can be parked safely on a steep incline, provided that the gear lever is not likely to jump into neutral (insure against this with rocks under the wheels.)

Crossing mountain passes

Driving in mountainous country is one of the most exhilarating parts of any journey. When climbing, keep the engine revving in a low gear; this way, the fan, water and oil pumps are kept working flat out to cool the engine and keep its bearings well-lubricated and lightly loaded. If the engine starts overheating, stop but keep it turning over fast for a few moments before switching off in order to get it below boiling point as quickly as possible. Pull off the road or, if you cannot, make sure you stop on a long straight and put your warning triangles up as quickly as possible. It is no joke for the driver of a heavy truck to find, on emerging from a blind bend, that he is head-on with another vehicle passing your own. Many people seem unaware of this danger.

When negotiating a pass, try to see where the road goes ahead of you. This should give you advance warning of oncoming vehicles. Large vehicles, which if local may be driven with panache, need the full width of the road to get round the bends, so be prepared to give way.

Drivers of right-hand-drive vehicles will often have to ask the passenger beside them to look up and round the curve when going into left-hand hairpins. Once it is known that the bend is clear, the vehicle should enter it as near to its outside edge as possible and then cut across in order to emerge on the correct side of the road. Always be in a position on entering the hairpin to permit hard acceleration around it for a good start on the next uphill straight.

Air horns should be used when overtaking lorries labouring up the pass, on the approach to blind bends or if there is livestock on the road ahead (but do not rely on the horn to clear them).

Long descents will soon overheat brakes if you rely on them excessively; the first sign of this, apart from a smell of hot asbestos, is reduced effectiveness. Never go fast down hills unless the bottom is in sight and you can run smoothly on to level ground or uphill. Use intermediate gears to restrain the vehicle and take some load off the brakes. Modern gearboxes allow swift changes, but double declutching into a low gear may be necessary if the vehicle has to be slowed following brake fade; the driver should be able to accomplish the movement reliably because in the event of complete brake failure a swift change down through the gears may be the only method of retaining control. Fast double declutching needs to be practised, as does the toe-and-heel technique of simultaneous operation of brake and accelerator.

Coasting in neutral downhill saves negligible fuel and leaves no other way of stopping if the brakes fade and a gear cannot be engaged; power-assisted brakes lose efficiency if the engine-powered servo unit is not operating.

If the brakes fail and the vehicle runs away, something which happens extremely rarely, it must be deliberately crashed as quickly as possible before it builds up more speed. Most mountain roads have an embankment or rock face on one side along which the driver must try to scrape in order to slow the vehicle. It is better to crunch up one side of the bodywork than to write off the whole vehicle and its occupants. Rally and racing drivers cultivate the habit of looking at the road ahead and planning emergency escape routes. There is always a risk of meeting someone on the wrong side of a blind bend, and if you have already made a mental note of an escape route it can mean the difference between a narrow shave and tragedy. This might sound unnecessarily cautious, but a driver who uses his imagination constructively is likely to be safer and more relaxed than one who does not. His passengers will feel confident in his ability, and will be able to enjoy the view without suffering the nervous tension that bad driving provokes.

Effects of high altitude

The atmosphere is thin at high altitudes, and an increased volume of air must be drawn into a vehicle's engine to maintain the supply of oxygen for combustion. Shortage of air causes loss of power, which means that a lower gear is needed for an incline which would not require it nearer sea level. High altitude upsets the efficiency of the carburettor, which is usually adjusted to produce the right fuel-air mixture at sea level and will therefore run rich (too much petrol) in the thin air found at, say, 10,000ft. An incorrect mixture increases an engine's breathing difficulties, so if you plan to do a lot of driving at altitudes over 7,000ft (2,000m), it may be worth fitting a smaller main jet to correct the balance. A number of manufacturers offer these as options or can advise which type should be fitted or carried as a spare; some carburettors compensate automatically for altitude. It is not a serious problem, however, and the author's experience in driving as high as 12,000ft is that a vehicle suffers no more than a tendency to overheat and the marked power loss already mentioned, with an unmodified carburettor.

A more serious high altitude problem with petrol engines is vapour lock, caused by petrol vaporising in the suction line to the fuel pump. Low pressure reduces the boiling points of all liquids, and if the engine gets very hot from climbing a pass the petrol may boil, causing fuel starvation, stalling and temporary starting difficulty. The only rapid cure is to soak a rag in water and drape it over the fuel pump, ensuring that it will not fall into the fan or on to the exhaust pipe. Diesels cannot suffer from vapour lock, but as they are size for size less powerful than a petrol equivalent their loss of power is more noticeable. Inefficient fuel combustion makes them smoke.

Extreme cold

Arctic conditions are encountered in some of the higher parts of Asia in winter and early spring; temperatures in the mountains of eastern Turkey fall below 0°F (about −18°C). Anti-freeze must be used or the radiator drained at night; never take a chance with the engine in sub-zero conditions. It is wise to park on a slope to allow a rolling start in the morning, when the engine oil will be thick and the battery less effective than usual.

In severe cold, diesel fuel thickens and many lorry drivers modify the exhaust system so that it blows hot gases over the main fuel tank.

Emergency manoeuvres

Skid avoidance is better than skid correction, and drivers should keep their eyes open for potential skid situations. Wet roads and ice are obviously slippery, but dead leaves, mud left by a vehicle driving on to the road from a dirt track, and loose gravel can be equally dangerous. Adverse camber or lack of camber on a bend can provoke a skid and so can the cobbles and tramlines common in many European cities. Vehicle faults can cause skidding, the most likely being a blowout at speed, fortunately rare with tubed radial tyres. A front tyre failure may lead to loss of steering, and braking compounds the difficulty. This is a good reason for keeping the best tyres on the front wheels (another is that good tyres are less likely to skid, and a front-wheel skid is more serious than a back-wheel slide). If a back tyre fails, hard braking will transfer some of the weight to the front wheels and you should be able to pull up in a fairly straight line.

Every motorist alarms himself sometimes by travelling too fast into a bend or on a slippery stretch where panic braking could cause loss of control; the best method to slow down rapidly is cadence braking, in which the pedal is pressed fairly hard in a series of short prods. It might lock the wheels momentarily, but they will be rotating again before the vehicle has time to change direction. Maximum tyre grip is obtained when the wheel is on the verge of skidding so a series of short, sharp applications of the brake will slow you down quicker than one long slide. This technique is best when there is a need to stop quickly on a slippery surface.

A driver should never get into the situation where he is going so fast that he cannot stop without hitting something, but it happens almost every time there is a pile-up on a motorway. The skilled driver can spin the vehicle by deliberately provoking a skid to turn it around on its axis; this absorbs a large part of the forward momentum, greatly increases the friction between tyres and road and might also allow an obstruction to be hit a glancing blow rather than head on. Spinning should be practised, and should not be experimented with for the first time in an emergency.

NAVIGATION

Someone who is keen on maps makes an ideal navigator, and his main function is to look after the maps, guide the driver through cities, find out as much as possible about places worth visiting and how to find them, and keep day-to-day records of mileage covered, fuel used and road conditions.

Outside Europe, choice of routes becomes limited as there may be a hundred miles between one main junction and the next, but if a wrong road is taken there may be no alternative to retracing steps. The navigator should never use guesswork, therefore.

The navigator should also check the frequency of fuelling points, especially in remote areas. Petrol company maps, AA and RAC itineraries and tourist office leaflets give a good guide, but trans-Saharan motorists are advised to check on the availability of fuel by asking travellers coming from the opposite direction, because garages sometimes run dry and the next tanker may not be due for a week. The navigator should always know the exact distance to the next and one or two subsequent fuelling points to avoid running out of fuel.

Trans-desert navigation by compass should never be attempted unless travelling in a well-equipped convoy with a local guide. In any case, to leave the marked tracks is prohibited, with good reason, in most Saharan countries. On the two main north–south routes through the Sahara, there are featureless wastes of flat gritty sand where the unwary could easily drive hundreds of miles off course. The main route is marked by oil drums or metal posts at kilometre intervals (although many are missing or have fallen over), and there is usually a distinct set of wheel tracks with numerous discarded tyres. If you have gone more than two or three kilometres without seeing markers or wheel marks, you should immediately retrace your tracks until you find definite evidence of being back on the main route. Be very wary of taking a short cut to the main track because you might drive over it without noticing. Never assume that an isolated set of wheel marks is the correct route; Touareg lorry drivers have an uncanny sense of direction and often drive across country, leaving misleading tracks, to visit isolated nomad encampments.

It is useful to make up parcels of maps for the main stages of the journey; frequently used maps such as the Michelin 153, 154 and 155 (Africa) survive better if kept folded in a see-through wallet.

Someone should make an effort to learn a few words of the main languages spoken along the route, and a basic vocabulary should include words for greeting, thanks, numbers, petrol, diesel, water, oil, yes, no, etc. Travellers will probably manage fairly well with English, but a display of even a smattering of their language usually pleases people and has the advantage of discouraging the exploitation of 'ignorant tourists'. French is useful in north and west Africa and German is often understood in Turkey and the Balkans.

Arabic script is used in nearly all countries from Morocco to Pakistan. Signposts and place names are usually repeated in Roman script so there is no great navigational problem, but the traveller in Iran may be confused when he first buys petrol as the pumps generally have Arabic numerals only. Some pump attendants have discovered that Europeans often do not know how much fuel has been put in, and a knowledge of numbers helps to avoid problems from this direction.

MAINTENANCE AND REPAIRS

There are plenty of guides to vehicle maintenance and repairs, and this section does not set out to paraphrase them or to tell the mechanic how to carry out routine work. At the same time, it recognises that some parties may not have the advantage of a fully skilled mechanic and that general advice based on overland experience may be useful. If some of the advice seems superfluous—a daily check of water, for example—it should be remembered that the vehicle is operating under harsh conditions and will require attention which at home might be safely put off until the weekend.

Maintenance

Each morning, check and top up the engine oil and water, inspect tyre treads and sidewalls for nails, stones and gashes, and take the pressures. Clean the windscreen and top up the washer. Look underneath for leaks of oil or water, and glance at the springs (look for broken leaves or U-bolts). Check propshaft bolts for tightness and inspect the spring shackles. If you have a Volkswagen or other air-cooled vehicle, see that the engine cooling fins are clean and unclogged. Look along the wheels and suspension to see if anything is distorted, and make a visual check of nuts and bolts for evidence of looseness. Carry out a similar visual check on the engine and note the condition and tension of the fan belt.

Whenever a stop is made during a trip along rough roads, do a quick inspection of the suspension and tyres. U-bolts, springs and shackles suffer a severe pounding on corrugated roads, and if (for example) one U-bolt has broken you can save further damage by replacing it immediately.

Investigate unusual symptoms and noises immediately. Noises usually fall into one of three categories: those which occur at engine speed frequency and are present whether the vehicle is moving or stationary (suspect things like tappets in need of adjustment, broken valve spring, weakness in bearings, generator, distributor, water pump); those which occur at wheel speed and are present when coasting with the engine switched off (suspect tyre damage, wheel bearings, prop shaft, rear axle, gearbox, speedometer drive, loose wheel nuts, clutch); those which occur in time with suspension or body movements (suspect a body, chassis or suspension fault).

Once a week, a more thorough inspection than usual is required. Change the air cleaner oil or element if there is visible contamination. Top up the battery and clutch and brake reservoirs and investigate undue loss of fluid immediately. Remove objects embedded in tyre treads and insects or grass seeds jammed in the radiator core. It is a good idea to plan the weekly check to coincide with a stay at a camp site where there are facilities for showering; the opportunity can be taken to do non-urgent jobs like oil changing, greasing and cleaning the vehicle while other members of the party look after other chores like washing clothes.

Clean and adjust the sparking plugs frequently to maximise performance, fuel economy and easy starting. Two-stroke sparking plugs have a tendency to whisker when poor petrol is used. If the engine was overhauled before departure, the cylinder head may need tightening down after about 500 miles, when the tappet clearances should be checked. Clean carburettor float chambers regularly; with diesels, be prepared to change filters often, taking great care to keep dust and dirt out of the system while doing so. With all engines, clean the fuel pump sediment chamber and gauze filter regularly.

Garages and service stations

Do not run much beyond the manufacturer's recommended service intervals, especially if driving a lot in heat, dust, sand or mud. Oil changing and greasing can be left to service stations in some areas, and many in Turkey and Iran are so efficient that they will quickly change the oil, grease everything that needs greasing and hose the vehicle underneath as well as on top, all for the cost of materials, plus a nominal charge. Always supervise servicing as well as all other garage work, pointing out which oil needs draining, how much new oil is needed and what grades should be used. Watch the old oil being drained out; if anything is about to go wrong with the gearbox or back axle, bits of metal coming out with the oil provide advance warning. See that the drain plugs are screwed up tight but not butchered by the wrong size of spanner. Check that grease is pumped into every grease point and that blocked nipples are cleaned or replaced, not passed over.

If the service station has a pit or hydraulic ramp, use the opportunity to have a close look at the underside of the vehicle, searching for hairline cracks in the chassis (which are easily welded if caught before they spread), oil leaks, loose nuts and bolts, damaged fuel and brake lines and electric cables.

When the oil filter element is being replaced, make sure that the filter housing is correctly seated. It is easy to put it back slightly crooked so that oil pours out at the joint when the engine is started.

Garage mechanics in Africa and Asia rarely mind being supervised, and if they do it is best to go elsewhere. It is usual for drivers in remote areas to oversee the maintenance of their vehicles. Mechanics are not always familiar with foreign vehicles and may value some guidance, and in any case it helps to establish a co-operative and friendly relationship. Sending one of the party to buy him a Coke is usually a popular move. It is also polite to give a tip of about 10 per cent of the cost of smaller jobs to the man who does the dirty work, unless he is the proprietor.

Ordinary service stations cannot usually do repair work and it is best to go to a specialist, who may work in an untidy shed behind a bazaar but will usually know exactly where to get spares and materials and have the experience to do a good job. Often, especially in Asia, one man does mechanical repairs, another does welding, another solders radiator leaks, someone

5   Stranded lorries (*above*) in Zambia's Western Province can provide worse obstacles than floods; (*centre*) normally dry or insignificant watercourses can quite suddenly swell into torrents—great care is needed though this diesel Transit in Afghanistan is not susceptible to wet ignition. (*Below*) Several tons of Land-Rover were safely punted with this Noah's Ark-inspired ferry across the Euphrates in Turkey.

else mends tyres, and so on. Once in the right part of town you need only point to whatever is wrong with the vehicle to be directed to the man for the job. Never let work start without agreeing a price; go elsewhere rather than fail to get a quotation. Once a price is agreed, you will be told if complications come to light which will cost more, and a new price must then be agreed. It often pays to be reluctant to accept the first quotation because, as in the bazaars, prices are flexible. If the repairs are going to be expensive and you are hard up, part-payment in kind in the form of spares, tools, a watch or transistor radio may be acceptable, but agreement must be made in advance.

Labour charges for repairs in Asia are usually less than half those charged in Europe, but the deep Sahara is very expensive as the few oases usually have only one mechanic whose monopoly may extend over thousands of square miles. Quotations may be two or three times what would be normal in Europe but vigorous haggling is recommended. Equatorial Africa is short of places for repairs except in main towns, where prices tend to be similar to those in Europe.

Some of the more motorised countries have secondhand or locally improvised parts for common types of vehicle, often quite cheap. The main routes through Asia have many places where repairs can be done and spares are available. India has severe import restrictions and imported spares are virtually unobtainable, but locally made parts are available for vehicles commonly used there. Indian mechanics are good at improvisation, as are repairers in most countries where foreign-made spares are scarce or expensive. Outside Europe, it is common to repair burnt-out electrical equipment such as generators and

6 The author's conversion of a rare foreward-control Land-Rover into a large enough and tough enough motorised caravan (*above*). Note the covered propane cylinders at the rear and the water tank filler on the side; the vehicle carried 15 gallons of water and 40 gallons of petrol in its tanks. Note the gas refrigerator, cooker and water pump inside (*below*) and the fan; the 12v fluorescent light uses hardly any current.

starter motors by rewinding, as opposed to the fitting of a new or reconditioned unit.

Breakdowns

If pressing repairs suddenly become necessary, try to find a firm, level, shady or sheltered place to stop, preferably with a water supply. If you buy a good quantity of petrol, a garage owner will rarely mind if you work in a convenient corner of his forecourt.

If forced to stop on the road in a potentially dangerous position, supplement your warning triangles with branches, jerrycans or other visible obstructions appropriately placed to give ample notice. Passengers should not leave the vehicle on the traffic side.

The vehicle may be towable, in which case attach a tow rope and try to persuade another driver to tow you to the nearest town. You must expect to pay for this service, particularly if the vehicle is a local lorry, and it may be as well to negotiate a price in advance.

Tyre troubles

The most frequent cause of enforced stoppage is a puncture. No one should ever get under a vehicle while it is jacked up; if on a hill, put rocks under the other wheels before jacking and lay the wheel flat once it is removed or it might roll away. Some vehicles have left-hand-thread nuts on the left-hand wheels; they are usually stamped LH or have diamond-shaped recesses machined in the corners.

If you intend to mend the puncture and have difficulty separating the tyre bead from the wheel rim, put the wheel flat under the vehicle and jack on to the tyre. If the only jack is already in use, remove it by supporting the axle on blocks. Do not throw away a tyre because it has been damaged internally as with a gaiter it may make an emergency spare. Home-made gaiters are available in the bazaars of most countries where new tyres are scarce or expensive. For safety's sake, avoid driving fast on a gaitered tyre. A worn but otherwise sound tyre can be remoulded fairly cheaply in many parts of Africa and Asia; a new tyre, if you can get one, may cost five times as much.

The best method of roadside puncture repair is the hot patch, easily obtainable in the east but less so in Europe where most punctures are vulcanised. Hot patches consist of a tin lid with the patch stuck on the back of it which is clamped to the inner tube with the G-clamp provided; a substance in the tin lid is ignited and heat-joins the patch far more effectively than rubber solution if done properly, ie with scrupulous degreasing and avoidance of finger contact.

Bodges and dodges

A workshop manual gives adequate advice on the diagnosis of engine troubles but none on how to improvise repairs in unusual situations, and it may not mention faults typical of hot or humid conditions. A common problem in damp places is poor connection at the battery terminals. The use of several high-powered driving lights in addition to headlights and other electrical units can overload the system and cause failure of generator and/or battery. Diode failure in alternators is not confined to harsh conditions but will if not noticed (ignition light shows) lead to a ruined battery. A fully charged battery will take an average vehicle about 1,000 miles provided that the use of electrically powered units, particularly the starter motor and headlights, is avoided or kept to an absolute minimum. Diesels will run indefinitely without a battery but re-starting may present problems as the glow plugs will not operate.

In the event of fuel pump failure, a can strapped to the roof and connected to the carburettor or injection pump (diesel) with plastic hose will suffice. If air has entered a diesel fuel line, as happens when you run out of fuel, it is necessary to prime the system before the engine will restart. Should a diesel fail to start because of a fault in the glow plug circuit or thermostart system, a squirt of ether-based aerosol such as Quickstart into the air intake should be sufficient to get you moving. Should diesel fuel congeal in cold conditions, apart from improvising some method of warming the fuel in the tank there is little that can be done but wait until the temperature rises; it is not uncommon for lorry drivers to light fires under their tanks, but this cannot be recommended.

A failed ignition switch can be by-passed by connecting a stout cable from the SW or BAT coil terminal to the large terminal on the starter motor or the non-earth terminal (the negative terminal on some vehicles, positive on others) of the battery. Disconnect it when you stop or the battery will drain. A non-essential switch on the dashboard could be used temporarily.

A clean ignition system—including the inside of the distributor head, and the rotor arm—minimises the risk of short circuits and facilitates inspection of the parts for the hairline cracks which can immobilise a vehicle by allowing tracking of the high tension current.

Overheating or oil pressure drop may indicate imminent engine seizure; if the driver suspects this, he should instantly depress the clutch and switch off, bringing the vehicle to rest with the brakes. A partial seizure may rectify itself, but the cause must be located and the fault cured. Gentle driving is necessary until the parts have bedded in. Total seizure must be followed by dismantling the engine, and major repairs are likely to be needed to restore it to normal. If only one cylinder is damaged, the connecting rod and piston can be removed completely but the cylinder must be deactivated by disconnecting the sparking plug, blocking the fuel supply and removing rockers or pushrods to keep the valves closed. Failure to disconnect the sparking plug would cause a serious explosion due to ignition of oil vapour in the sump. This bodge is sufficient only as a means of helping a badly damaged vehicle to limp towards assistance. A 6-cylinder vehicle may run on four cylinders.

The most common problem with brakes is the gradual loss of fluid through the wheel cylinder seals, and the only cure is to replace them. Never use an unknown brand of fluid as it may be incompatible with your system and ruin the seals completely. If much brake fluid is lost, a desperate emergency can be met with soapy water containing a generous amount of washing-up liquid, but the system must be dismantled and thoroughly flushed after. In the event of damage to a brake pipe feeding one or both back wheels, or to the brakes themselves, the pipe could be cut and sealed; if there is damage to a front brake, the back brakes could be cannibalised and sealed—the cut end of pipe hammered flat and securely crimped over with pliers and checked for leaks, while another person depresses the brake pedal. The driver must then drive well within the reduced braking capacity.

Clutch slip—which may be caused simply by bad adjustment—can sometimes be cured if caused by oil leakage by depressing the clutch pedal and, with engine running, tipping a bottle of carbon tetrachloride or squirting a liquid fire extinguisher into the housing to dissolve the oil. Talcum powder or fuller's earth will give the worn lining some bite. If no spare is available, new friction material can be riveted to the existing unit, perhaps cut from scrapped lorry clutches.

Broken spring leaves can sometimes be effectively bound by wrapping them in wet uncured leather which, as it dries, shrinks and makes a tight joint. If a rear spring breaks forward of the axle, the axle may shift and pull the handbrake on, in which case disconnect the cable. If chassis and broken spring are in contact, liberal greasing will reduce friction; otherwise, place a wooden block between the axle and the chassis and proceed at walking pace. Where it is impossible to improvise on the spot, the broken parts must be taken to the nearest town where spares, repairs and—ideally—retempering are available. Spring leaves can be welded, and blacksmiths in areas of untarred roads regard spring repair and leaf replacement and manufacture as commonplace.

After an accident, ensure that vital parts are undamaged; if they are, they should obviously have prompt attention. Body damage can be treated temporarily with a hammer to get bent bits out of the way of moving parts and sharp edges into a safe condition. If you are without a windscreen, drive with the side windows shut.

Some Problems

PEOPLE PROBLEMS

Fellow passengers
A small group of people travelling for some time will generally not avoid friction, and one difficult person can create chaos and exaggerate everyone's tensions. Subordination to a leader goes against the grain for most, but it helps if there is somebody to have the last word in a dispute and give direction when decisions have to be made. By common consent, the natural leader is usually the initiator, organiser, or someone experienced in overland travel. It is well worth assigning responsibilities to everyone in an overland trip of more than two or three, as a casually organised journey will become chaotic; some people will do everything and resent others who sit around doing nothing, who in turn will resent the busybodies who seem to do everything.

Pre-departure discussion of possible causes of friction should help to prevent squabbling en route, and the early and good-humoured airing of grievances should be encouraged.

A common cause of friction is too ambitious an itinerary for the time available. It helps if all members accept the same return schedule, or some may want to hurry while others take their time. The main advantage overland trips have over long voyages in small boats is that people can wander off on their own or in small groups, and time should be allowed for this.

Money can cause trouble, particularly as personal budgets vary. All costs must be seen to be shared fairly and anything that does not have to be shared, like meals in restaurants, is best paid for individually. Separate bills allow the hungry or thirsty to indulge while those trying to economise can do so without embarrassment.

Privacy can be a problem. Particularly at the start of a trip, girls often find it embarrassing to ask the driver for a loo stop. Passengers seem to need to stop more often than drivers, so whoever is driving should find a suitable place at regular intervals. If driving through desert or open grasslands, look for a bridge or culvert under the road; most desert roads are raised on a slight embankment and watercourses usually pass through corrugated steel or concrete pipes big enough to walk into for complete privacy. Seasoned travellers always carry a small supply of toilet paper in a pocket, particularly in Asia where it is rarely supplied.

Local people and customs

Mature overlanders take people they come into contact with along their route as they find them, and do not expect special treatment. They allow for the fact that local and national ways of life differ from those which they know and may seem unusual or even disagreeable, but they realise that as brief visitors they must remain detached. It is the experience of the author that rural people are almost everywhere hospitable and straight-forward; they will make it plain if they like you and equally plain if they do not. If a bad impression has been left by an earlier party, the assumption that your group will be obnoxious is forgivable and may be difficult to dispel. In areas where outsiders are few, you will almost certainly be offered the hospitality traditional among unsophisticated people all over the world. This is usually the case away from the well-worn tourist routes—for example, in tropical Africa.

The level of friendliness has unfortunately deteriorated during the last few years along the main routes to the east and is most marked in parts of Turkey where formerly travellers were the recipients of help and kindness; the same pattern is appearing along the tourist trail to India.

This book is mainly for the traveller (as opposed to the

tourist) who will journey in remote places as well as along the well-beaten track, and it will not be considered patronising if the need is stressed for thoughtfulness and understanding, which can do so much to increase friendship between peoples and continents. A single unruly group will leave a trail of ill-feeling that a dozen diplomats will not be able to remedy.

It is important to take note of local customs, and if one of them is hospitality it should be borne in mind that the host may be poor; a reciprocal gift such as coffee, canned fruit or cigarettes is an acceptable way of saying thank you. Sugar lumps are a luxury in the Sahara and are appreciated by the Touareg, and children anywhere seem to like sweets and chocolate.

In some countries (Iran, for example) it is not considered polite to accept something when it is first offered, and even a cigarette should be offered several times.

Sensitivity over poverty is understandably common, and there may be resentment if too much interest is taken in beggars and shanty towns, for example. Politics is another sensitive area, and nothing should be done or said which could be taken as a slight on a political leader; it could land you in jail.

Most women in Islamic countries are kept out of sight and are always demurely dressed or even veiled in public, and western girls who insist on wearing revealing mini-skirts, tight trousers or shorts will almost certainly attract unpleasant attention. Young men may try to pinch or bump into them and older men might spit at their feet. The centres of some Moslem cities are now so westernised that emancipated local girls wear the latest fashions, but they know how to deal with abuse and they also know how far they can stretch their emancipation. Some remote areas such as central Afghanistan are potentially dangerous for revealingly dressed girls, and one bikini-clad swimmer in the lake at Band-i-Amir was shot dead by a hill tribesman; she affronted his ideas of dress and she was defiling the lake, which had religious significance. The same fate met a couple who went swimming in the nude in a Turkish lake. Brief clothes can be safely worn in tourist areas such as hotel grounds and camp sites, but usually nowhere else in western Asia. India and most of Africa are more tolerant of unconventional or minimal clothing, except currently Malawi and Uganda where mini-skirts are banned.

Men can cause offence to Moslems by wearing shorts, particularly in areas near mosques or in pilgrim centres, but shorts are generally accepted as informal wear from Pakistan eastwards and from the Sahara southwards.

It is particularly important to dress respectably when visiting mosques and temples, and women are normally expected to cover their arms and wear knee-length dresses or trousers with a tunic. Men should wear long trousers. Shoes usually have to be left at the entrance where an attendant looks after them and expects a small tip. In some cases women must be veiled, and a veil can often be hired.

Public demonstrations of affection between the sexes will cause offence in Moslem countries.

Alcohol should be drunk discreetly; good wines and beers are produced in Turkey, Iran and Afghanistan but are disapproved of by a large proportion of the population particularly in the latter two countries. It is not tactful to eat in public during the thirty days of *Ramadan* when devout Moslems fast.

Officialdom

Overlanders will meet mainly the customs/immigration officers, and a member of the party should be chosen as the border crossing negotiator. An apparently well-organised and respectable party need not expect undue delay or trouble provided documents are in order and questions can be answered satisfactorily. Nevertheless, the negotiator may need to call on reserves of patience and persistence and it pays to prepare in advance for on-the-spot document-filling. When entering and leaving non-European countries, all travellers usually have to fill in a card which requires passport number, place and date of birth, name, and so on. The quickest way to deal with this is for one or two people to fill in the lot from a prepared list; individual cards should then be placed inside the appropriate passports and handed to the immigration officer. Check that the correct passports are returned. Meanwhile, the party should wait in the vehicle and should not wander around the border post.

Co-operate in case of a vehicle search, which will not usually be detailed unless there is a suspicion that you may be running drugs, with which there is a far greater customs preoccupation than with wines, spirits and watches. Young people who have come overland from Afghanistan, Nepal and Morocco are vulnerable. The only and absolute rule is never to have anything to do with the oriental drug scene; penalties are exceedingly harsh, and what starts as a lark may end as a serious matter. Persons carrying more than 1kg of hashish face execution if caught in Iran, and a year's imprisonment for every gram of lesser amounts. The risk of being caught is high, particularly as some customs posts have dogs trained to sniff out drugs.

If requested, travellers must open and unpack their luggage and be prepared to explain the contents.

It is pointless to indicate that you are in a hurry to cross a border, but many posts close at sunset or 18.00 hours local time and may speed up procedures for late arrivals in order to shut on time.

Contact with the police may arise from an unwitting infringement of a local traffic regulation, and if innocence is the case innocence can reasonably be pleaded. Lack of understanding due to absence of a common language may, if the offence is trivial, make the officer decide that it is pointless to pursue the matter.

All officials must be treated with respect, but if you think you have cause for complaint be insistent and if necessary try to speak to a person of higher rank. Take care never to place an official in a position where he will lose face if he co-operates with you; it is better to lose face yourself than to start a confrontation which you will not win.

Other overlanders

Much can be learned from other overlanders, particularly those coming the other way, and on a long trip the same groups may meet several times. In remote areas with little traffic, it is customary to compare notes with those you meet; on busier roads, you meet on camp sites and at places of interest, or where routes converge and cross such as the Bosporus, Algeciras, New Delhi and Nairobi.

Security should never be relaxed, even at crowded camp sites with a perimeter fence; there is a real danger that a tiny minority of dishonest overlanders will take advantage of the carelessness of others who leave valuables lying around.

The Algerian government insists that normal vehicles should cross the Sahara only by the main routes and then in convoy with at least one lorry or 4-wheel-drive vehicle. Algerian lorry drivers generally refuse to have much to do with obviously inadequate vehicles, and other overlanders are co-opted. Even Land-Rover clutches do not stand up indefinitely to pulling other vehicles out of sand in very hot conditions, yet if responsibility has been taken for shepherding less-suitable vehicles they cannot be abandoned. If you are heavily loaded or have reservations, however small, it is best to deter potential convoy-formers from the start.

CAMPING

Finding a camp site
Once in remote areas you will no longer find organised camp sites or hotels at convenient intervals. It is important to look for a camp site well before darkness falls because in tropical latitudes dusk and twilight are brief and it is completely dark soon after the sun goes down. Once it is dark, not only is it much more difficult to find a good place to pitch tents but cooking and all the other camp chores become much harder and in mosquito areas insects become troublesome.

The search for a site should begin at some predetermined time, say half an hour before sunset, when every place must be investigated until a suitable one is found. Obviously, the nature of the terrain will influence the time needed to search. Do not camp on the fringes of a town or village unless you can get permission to use enclosed private ground or there is some suitable open space such as a municipal park; you may wake up to find yourself in the middle of a market. The fringes of some large cities can be hazardous after dark and although Istanbul, Tehran, Kabul and Tangier have areas of open space, mostly in the poorer quarters, it would be most unwise to camp in them without placing armed guards. Villages and small country towns are predominantly safe; the greatest risk is of attracting a large and inquisitive audience.

Dry river beds are notorious as bad camp sites because of the flood risk, something to be wary of in mountain areas where there is melting snow or the possibility of rain, but there is no real risk in arid regions where in fact dry river beds may be the only flat spaces soft enough to take tent pegs. If camping in hilly or mountainous terrain, avoid the base of steep slopes where there is a danger of falling rocks.

Animal tracks are to be avoided if you do not wish to be woken by livestock moving at dawn to its grazing grounds. If you plan to camp by a busy main road, try to find a spot where you will not be visible to passing vehicles; much of the lorry traffic in hot countries travels at night and passing lorry drivers may offer a greeting on their air horns.

Avoid sites within a mile of marshy ground or stagnant water which are breeding places for mosquitoes and other nocturnal biting insects. Whenever possible, find a patch of high ground or drive a few miles away from a lake or large river. In areas where you feel it may be dangerous to camp in open country, approach the local police for advice; they may even allow you to camp in their compound and use their lavatories and water supply. Army camps are usually too security-conscious to allow strangers to camp or use their facilities but most rural garage owners with large premises will let you camp in a corner of the forecourt; modern filling stations often have clean toilets and sometimes a shower.

In crowded areas it is difficult to camp anywhere on open ground without attracting a huge audience. The solution in India is to go to the nearest dak bungalow, which is usually equipped with several suites of bedrooms and usually has a garden or walled yard. It is possible to spend the night inside cheaply, and if you prefer to camp or sleep in the vehicle the *chowkidar* will usually allow you to do so free or for a nominal charge and will let you use the shower or bathroom and prepare a meal for you for very low payment. Almost every town and some large villages have a dak bungalow (which is usually clearly signposted) and the same kind of system is used in Pakistan and some Commonwealth countries in Africa, as well as in Asia.

Dangers—real and imaginary

The world is safer than the news media would have us believe, but there are undoubtedly some areas where only the foolish or the well-armed travel or stop at night. Most are forbidden to ordinary travellers as governments do not want foreigners to fall foul of their internal problems. It is advisable to check on the situation before driving at night or camping in remote parts of Afghanistan and Pakistan, and known trouble spots should of course be avoided. If in doubt, ask the local police; tourist offices and embassy officials are often ill-informed about the remoter parts of their country and may play safe by being unnecessarily cautious. Tourist offices exist largely to promote the developed areas and will therefore do their best to keep visitors from other parts.

To some extent the safety of a party depends on its makeup. Small groups or groups consisting mostly of girls are clearly more vulnerable than a dozen men who would probably be able to camp almost anywhere without much risk. Sleepers are more exposed in tents than in a vehicle.

Animals present few problems. Wolves and bears roam the wildest parts of Asia but avoid human habitation except in the depths of winter when hunger might bring them out of the mountains. In Africa, few game areas are not designated as reserves, in which camping is controlled. Outside the reserves, a leopard might attack a lone person walking well away from the vehicle or camp. Hyenas have been known to bite a sleeping person so it is best to sleep in a vehicle or tent. Lighting a camp fire or burning an electric light all night will normally scare creatures off.

The danger of being bitten by a dog is not great, but rabies is endemic in large areas of the world and even a lick from a rabid dog can transmit this extremely dangerous disease. A rabid dog may look quite healthy, and the only absolutely safe course is to avoid having any contact with dogs. If anyone is bitten by a dog that might be rabid, they should get immediate medical attention and a course of anti-rabies injections unless the animal has been vaccinated against rabies.

Insects are a great nuisance and hazard, and the best precaution is an effective liquid repellent; creams are rather messy. It may help while cooking and eating to set up a bright light as a decoy; a Tilley lamp with a mantle is ideal. Contrary to popular belief, a smoky fire does not repel insects except actually within the smoke.

Scorpions can be a danger on dry stony ground as they normally live under large flat stones or in holes in the ground. Never put your hand into a hole in the ground in desert areas, and turn over stones with your foot (but not if you are wearing sandals). Shake out shoes that have been left on the ground overnight.

Snakes are often feared by people setting off for the first time to Africa or Asia, but they are timid creatures and are rarely seen by motorised travellers. After three years in central Africa and travels of over 100,000 miles in hot countries, the author has seen snakes in the wild only half-a-dozen times, and there was never any risk of being bitten. Snakes could be a danger if surprised or cornered in thick undergrowth or jungle, but if the walker moves slowly and noisily, the snakes (which usually have acute hearing but poor eyesight) will move out of the way.

Statistically, the most dangerous creature in hot climates is the mosquito, and it is worth repeating the importance of a course of anti-malaria pills.

EATING

It is possible to live entirely on restaurant meals in Asia whereas the trans-African traveller must take food and cooking facilities. However, trans-Asian travellers can economise by cooking for themselves. Evening meals in restaurants can be supplemented by lunches of *nân* (unleavened bread) and kebabs, or processed cheese brought from home. French loaves can be bought in Saharan oases and conventional white bread in towns further south; stored immediately in a polythene bag, bread stays edible for up to 24 hours. Exposed, it goes hard and dry within an hour or two in a desert climate. Pâté is available in most French-speaking areas, and a small tin, some bread, a mug of tea and perhaps some dates make an adequate Saharan lunch for most people.

Although self-catering parties will normally stock up with adequate supplies of tinned and freeze-dried food before leaving Europe, certain items will need replenishing during the journey and fresh fruit and vegetables should be used to supplement meals whenever possible. Vegetables considered expensive and exotic in Europe are often cheap while more homely produce is unavailable or expensive. Peppers, aubergines (egg plant), courgettes, gem squash and ladies' fingers are commonly found in the arid countries of the Middle East and northern Africa, onions and tomatoes seem to be universal, but potatoes, cabbage, beans and other common European vegetables are less easy to find. Rice, sugar, salt, flour and other staples are available all the year round in most areas. Chicken eggs can be bought almost everywhere and make a cheap, convenient and safe supplement to your stores. Citrus fruits, grapes and other Mediterranean fruits can often be bought (in season) from Turkey right through to India. Iran, Afghanistan and Pakistan produce melons during the summer. In India and tropical Africa, you will find exotic fruits such as mangoes, avocado pears, pineapples, paw paw or papaya (the African and Asian names respectively), coconuts (along the coasts) and of course bananas. Bananas are so plentiful and cheap in some areas that it pays to develop new recipes for them other than eating them straight from the skin; banana fritters make a popular and cheap sweet which keeps quite well and therefore doubles as a snack for eating on the move.

Supplies bought during the journey can be stored in spaces

vacated as other food is used. Plastic containers should be used for spillable commodities.

Meat is often available, and even though standards of hygiene in some bazaar butchers' shops leave a little to be desired you need not close your mind to buying it. Good steaks in some parts of Africa cost a quarter of the European price. Do not buy pork except in areas where you can be confident that the pigs have been hygienically reared. Pork may carry dangerous parasites which cause appalling illnesses (hence the religious taboos against eating it). If you buy what you judge to be safe pork, it is vital to cook it thoroughly just in case as the parasites are very resistant to heat.

Freezing does not kill bacteria; ice cubes made from unsafe water will contaminate a drink.

The kitty organiser should go shopping when necessary, and as prices are mostly negotiable this will mean haggling.

WATER

Water is so heavy that even the minimum necessary quantity can account for a large proportion of a vehicle's load. Opinion on the quantity needed varies as much as the degree of economy different people can achieve; the requirement will be greatest in waterless regions where, in case of a breakdown, sufficient reserves for several days must be provided, even on a main through-route. Anyone venturing into remoter areas must carry even better reserves. Whatever the eventuality, the aim should be to arrive at the next water supply with a small reserve still on board, because it is essential to be prepared for a delay such as a breakdown a few miles short of the supply. The risk

7   The Volkswagen Kombi is popular for overlanding (*above*); it is rugged and has above-average ground clearance. Two different models are seen driving through southern Morocco for Spanish Sahara. Another suitable vehicle is the Land-Rover (*below*); its spares are virtually a negotiable currency in many parts. Here the author's diesel negotiates a Saharan wadi—note the obvious soft spots to be avoided.

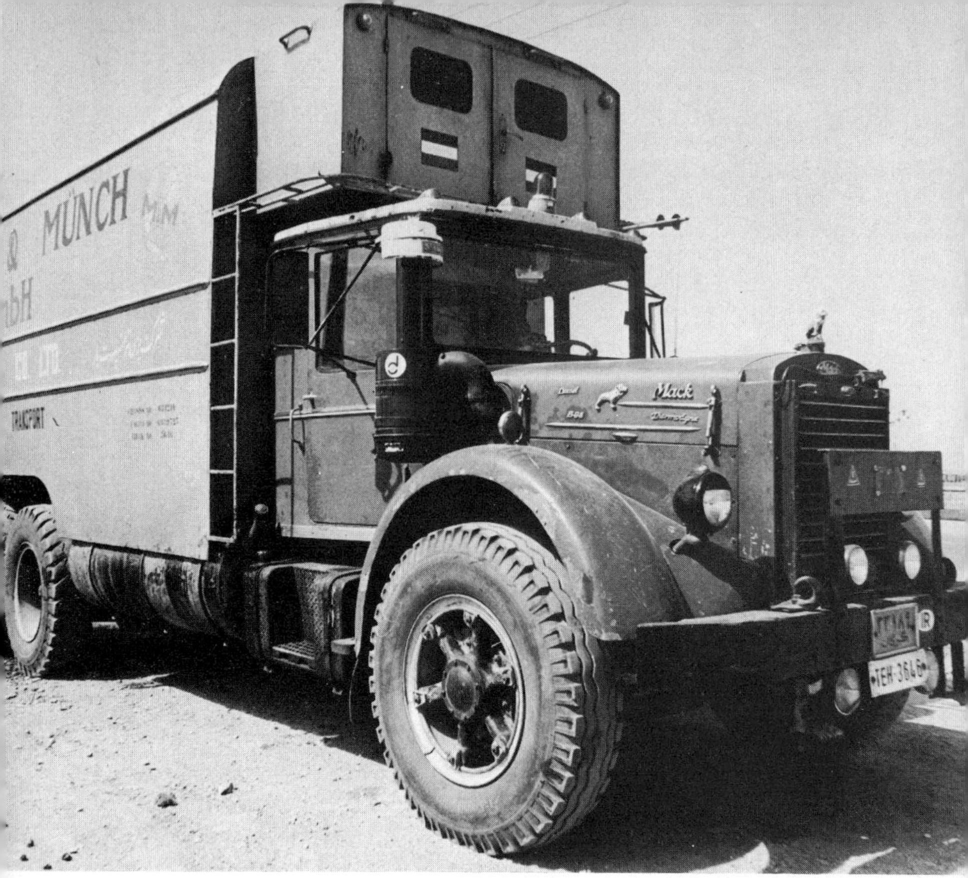
MÜNCH
Mack
TEH-3646

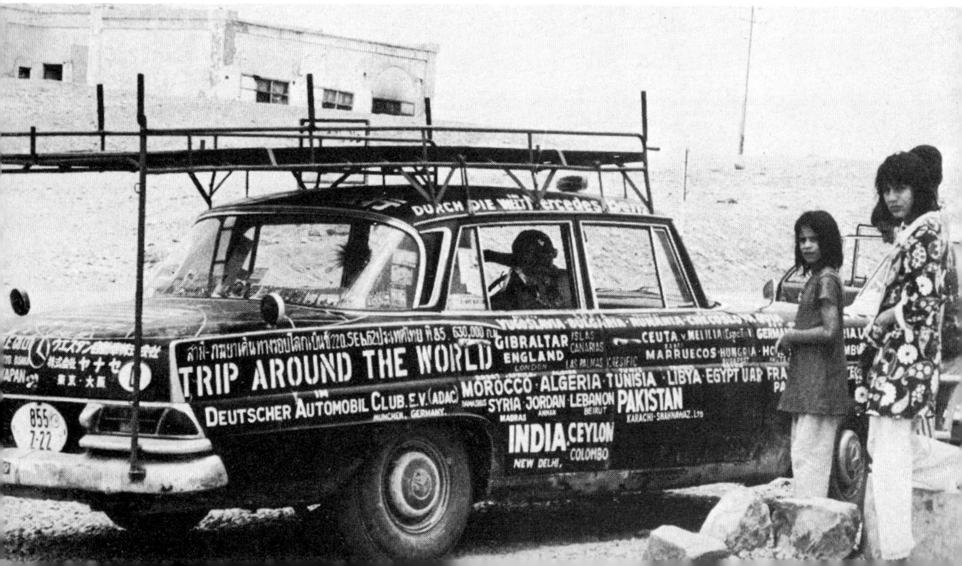
DURCH DIE WELT
TRIP AROUND THE WORLD
DEUTSCHER AUTOMOBIL CLUB.E.V.(ADAC)
GIBRALTAR
ENGLAND
MOROCCO · ALGERIA · TUNISIA · LIBYA · EGYPT UAR
SYRIA · JORDAN · LEBANON
PAKISTAN
INDIA, CEYLON
NEW DELHI,
COLOMBO
CEUTA
MARRUECOS
JAPAN

of dying of thirst on one of the main trans-Saharan routes is negligible during the winter season when there is sufficient traffic to rescue you, but as you will probably want to repair the vehicle on the spot (getting a tow can be extremely expensive) and cannot normally beg water off passing travellers you must have enough to last an extra day or two.

Water requirement must be balanced against the danger of overloading your vehicle. *A Traveller's Guide to Health* suggests ten pints (six litres) per day as an average requirement in a tropical climate, plus an extra pint (half litre) for every hour of activity. Two gallons per person per day, or a jerrycan for two people per day, should be sufficient for washing (lightly), cooking and drinking. A complete radiator refill should be carried in addition.

Water usage must be controlled in accordance with the ease of replenishment. Vital usage is for drinking and the engine, plus a strictly limited amount for cooking. When water is easily obtained it is reasonable to allow the luxury of an individual bowl for washing, but when it is scarce the rule should be a communal bowl for hand-washing and a mugful for each person for face-washing. Travellers in dry climates usually feel less dirty than in humid areas; dust brushes off, and in any case it is usually possible to get a good wash at the next oasis.

Drinking can be reduced safely by taking a small amount frequently; it is unhealthy and wasteful to go too long without water and then drink a great quantity.

Salt as well as water is lost by the body in hot climates and a danger of losing too much is that thirst sensations decrease and lead to insufficient water intake. Lack of salt often gives rise to symptoms of heat exhaustion and extreme thirst even when adequate water has been taken, and it is therefore important to take salt tablets or eat something like a salty soup with the evening meal (this is usually enjoyable when the

8 Big and ambitious competition! An Iranian heavy lorry and a graffitied Mercedes.

body is short of salt). Watch for signs of heat exhaustion in people who are apparently not drinking enough; it can strike suddenly. The cure is plenty of liquid, salt and rest in cooler conditions (a damp towel wrapped around the head helps). Acclimatisation will help reduce water consumption because people will drink less and learn to use it sparingly.

Water purification

Water supplies in many parts of Asia, Africa and some parts of southern Europe are contaminated; doubtful water should always be purified before drinking. Official camp sites sometimes have two water supplies, one for drinking and one for washing. A few cities have safe chlorinated supplies (Tehran and most of the bigger Iranian cities and some Turkish towns). Afghanistan, India and most other Asian countries have dangerous piped supplies; local people may be seen drinking water, but this does not indicate that it is safe. Dysentery, cholera, polio, hepatitis and other waterborne diseases are often endemic and watermains are liable to contamination by sewers. Less densely populated Africa is generally better supplied with safe water, and unsafe supplies are not so likely to be infected with such dangerous diseases as are found in Asia. Water from deep artesian wells in the Sahara can often be safely drunk unpurified if it is intercepted where it is piped out of the ground. El Goléa has excellent piped water; In Salah has a safe but slightly brackish source in the palmery; Tamanrassat, Agadés, Gao, Tessalit, Reggane and Adrar have (to the author's knowledge) piped supplies which should be sterilised. Do not rely on getting water from roadside oasis wells marked on the Michelin and other maps as they are often dry, silted up, or contain filthy water. Crystal-clear water cascading down a mountainside is rarely as clean as it looks and should never be drunk unpurified unless it is just emerging from a deep spring; sheep and goats commonly infect water with a number of dangerous bugs. Even mountain snow can be dangerous unless freshly fallen; old Himalayan snows often contain a number of organisms.

Certain parasites can be picked up through the skin, the most common being bilharzia which infects most slow-moving or stagnant water in tropical Africa and the various forms of hookworm found in India and Africa. Never wade or swim in any water in Africa within a mile or so of reeds or rushes (where the snail breeds which carries bilharzia) and never walk barefoot in a muddy or slimy area in Africa or Asia where people and animals have walked. If you think you may have picked up infection, a medical examination on your return is essential because the effects may not show for months or even years.

Decontaminating water

The most reliable method of sterilisation is to boil it vigorously for at least ten minutes; this will kill even the most hardy bacteria. It is not a practical method for producing drinking water but safe tea, coffee and soup can be made. Tea bought in oriental *chai-khanas* is invariably safe to drink. Luxury hotels in India have water boilers for producing large quantities of drinking water, and kitchen staff may be willing to fill cans even if you are not staying at the hotel. The staff of dak bungalows will often boil water for a small fee, but it should be seen to be properly boiled.

The most convenient method of water purification is to use sterilising tablets, dropping the recommended dose into each container of drinking water each time it is filled. They are not proof against all contamination but are normally effective provided that the water is reasonably clean. The dose can be increased if the water gives cause for concern. Boots the chemists sell effective and inexpensive own-brand sterilising tablets and there are other commercially produced preparations including some which claim effectiveness within only ten minutes. Alternatively, a pharmacist could prepare quantities of stabilised bleach powder, measured to suit the size of your water containers, which is more economical than tablets for large parties. It is important to take an adequate supply of sterilising tablets as they are almost impossible to buy in many of the countries where they are likely to be needed. Economy can be practised by keeping two water supplies, one sterilised and the other not, but they must be clearly distinguishable. If unsafe water is used to top up the safe supply, even a small amount, all will have to be resterilised.

Standard sterilising tablets and stabilised bleach need time to take effect, which is inconvenient if you are very thirsty. In restaurants, order soft drinks in factory-sealed bottles or drink tea; if you prefer water, carry a small dropper bottle of tincture of iodine. Two or three drops make a glass of water safe in about five minutes but amounts of more than a few drops are harmful. Apart from this, it gives an antiseptic taste. (This tip came from a US Peace Corps medic in Katmandu, Nepal—perhaps the most hazardous place for contracting illness from water.)

Water can be effectively purified by filters designed to remove particles so fine that even bacteria are caught. Several firms market filtering devices but a filter capable of coping with the quantities of water needed by a large party will be expensive, and fairly slow in use. Filtration with good equipment is as effective as boiling but has the additional advantages of needing neither fuel nor post-treatment cooling.

Decontaminating vegetables and fruit

Vegetables and fruit handled and displayed on a bazaar or market stall should be thoroughly soaked in an antiseptic solution, the cheapest and most convenient being potassium permanganate crystals (permanganate of potash) in water—just enough to turn the water pale mauve. Alternatively, peel all fruit including grapes and take care to prevent the peel from touching the parts to be eaten. Fruits with hard skins, such as apples, should be reasonably safe if they are clean in the first place and then washed and polished, but the furry skins of peaches may harbour bacteria. Though tedious, these precautions are important and no person should disregard them. A moment's carelessness can cause misery and disruption which may affect the remainder of the journey.

In Asia, beware of salads. Only the most exclusive restaurants go to the trouble of sterilising lettuce, and if the local water is unsafe the lettuce will be equally so. Tempting though a salad may be, make your own or stick to cooked local specialities.

The traveller cannot hope to screen out every germ, only to minimise the risk of infection, and the seasoned traveller builds up resistance by gradual exposure. With so much enjoyment and new experience at stake, risks with food and water are not worth taking.

HAGGLING

Once away from the land of supermarkets you enter a world where nearly all prices are negotiable. Whether buying an egg in a village bazaar or arranging expensive vehicle repairs, you will invariably have to haggle.

It is normal practice in much of Africa and Asia for a shopkeeper to ask two or three times the price he is prepared to accept, which should be countered by an offer of a quarter or a third of his asking price and followed by haggling to reach a compromise, both sides pleading dramatic reasons for needing to sell/buy at a high/low price. The average successful bazaar salesman will rapidly size up a customer and decide what sort of price is applicable; he will watch for signs of impatience or over-keenness which may allow him to get a better price by using delaying tactics. Buyers wanting to haggle something down to a low price should therefore take their time and avoid showing much enthusiasm. It may help to ask the prices of a lot of different items so that the dealer is not sure what is really sought. It is not important to haggle for ages over small purchases but it can be well worth taking trouble over negotiations for expensive items, even to the extent of visiting the same shop several times on different occasions, restarting the negotiations at the figure arrived at during the previous visit.

If your mind is set on a particular item you should discover its general price range by making enquiries elsewhere; ignorance in this respect will put you at a disadvantage. However, as an enquiry about price indicates to most eastern bazaar salesmen a wish to buy, you may cause perplexity if you offer your thanks and walk away.

When ordering any kind of service, such as repair work or even a taxi ride, always ask for a quotation and haggle a price in advance. Once a firm price has been agreed, it is most unlikely that a dealer will attempt to change it; similarly, the buyer has a responsibility to keep his side of the deal, paying immediately for work done unless there is genuine cause for complaint. If a price is not agreed in advance, a buyer may be considered so wealthy that price is unimportant to him, an attitude that invites overcharging. This applies particularly to taxis; meters, where fitted, may be rigged or out of order and the driver should be asked for at least an estimate before the journey begins. A local resident may be able to give an indication of a fair price. Taxis are cheap in many Asian cities and it may be good policy to leave the overland vehicle locked in the municipal camp site and travel locally by taxi.

When haggling in the east, the potential purchaser may be offered a chair and a glass of *chai* so that negotiations can be carried out in comfort. It is polite to accept; hurried, rude westerners have done much harm to the image of travellers. Lack of a common language is not necessarily a drawback as an interpreter will usually be sent for if necessary, and English and French are widely known in any case. Much can be accomplished with sign language or sketches and figures on paper or even scratched in the dust on the ground.

EMERGENCIES

Those contemplating an overland trip are usually concerned about the dangers that must be faced, to judge by the questions that are most frequently asked, and it is admitted that experienced overlanders sometimes have qualms about the wisdom of visiting certain places or indulging in certain activities en route. There are trouble spots, but most can be avoided; there are potentially awkward situations, but most can be recognised before they boil over.

Safety belts

Safety belts, ideally of the inertia reel type because they allow freedom of movement, undoubtedly reduce the risk of injury in a crash but also allow the driver to carry out violent avoiding action or braking without throwing his passengers about. Passengers wearing belts are more comfortable when travelling on rough roads as they have less need to brace themselves against the movement of the vehicle.

Crash helmets and eye protection

Motorcyclists must protect head and eyes. Crash helmets are essential in hot countries because in addition to their obvious use they guard against heatstroke; the danger may seem small to a rider who is enjoying the blast of air as he travels, but the sun is usually strong enough to affect him after a short exposure. Goggles or visors protect against impact by large insects—a locust or swarm of bees—and loose material thrown up by other vehicles, all of which can be damaging if caught in the face.

Road accidents

As at home, vigilance is essential everywhere. Pedestrians are a hazard and it is wise, and not considered antisocial, to use the horn in long blasts when driving through busy streets. If you are unfortunate enough to hit and injure a pedestrian, be aware that bystanders may react violently; in some places where traffic is light the police advise a motorist to drive straight to the police station without attempting to stop. A road accident may have a traumatic effect on a simple community and a driver and his passengers could risk serious hurt or even death if caught. If the accident occurs where there are few witnesses, the only possible course of action is to stop and render first aid and if necessary take the victim to hospital with a friend or relative to reassure him. If an apparently angry crowd gathers, leave immediately and drive to the police station.

An accident must always be reported, both as an almost universal legal requirement and because not to do so could be taken as an admission of guilt. It is wrong to assume that you will get away without being apprehended; even in remote areas, communications are better than you think they are.

Where there is no prospect of summoning an ambulance, either commandeer the first vehicle to take the victim to the nearest hospital or contact a police or army post, which may have suitable transport and trained personnel. Most remote police or army posts have a medical officer and may be able to call for a helicopter or light aircraft in an emergency.

In case of a collision with another vehicle, avoid moving either until the police arrive. Put up warning triangles and take further measures necessary to prevent a multiple pile-up, and if possible take a set of photographs of the crash scene from all angles, preferably in black and white which can be processed quickly. If the other vehicle's driver is to blame, make it plain that you consider that the fault lies with him and try to get witnesses who will explain what happened when the police arrive.

In India, to kill or injure a cow is considered almost as serious as maiming a person, and a traveller who hits a cow should drive immediately to the police station to report the matter; no attempt must be made to negotiate with people on the spot. The black Indian water buffalo is not in the same category as the cow as far as accidents are concerned.

Breakdowns in remote areas

If you get lost or break down in a featureless desert area (in practice, likely only in the Sahara), stay by or in the vehicle and do not start walking. A vehicle is a much more obvious target for searchers than a lone walker. You should have notified the police before setting out, and it is likely that an investigation will start when you are overdue at your destination (if you have lost contact with an accompanying vehicle, it is assumed that you will be searched for or reported missing).

Marine flares or smoke signals could be carried against this emergency, and an electronic flashgun is a possible position indicator at night; during the day, make your position as conspicuous as you can by spreading brightly coloured tents and gear around.

Explorers on foot, mountaineers, and those traversing the Sahara from east to west presumably know what risks they are taking and do not set out lightheartedly; a knowledge of survival techniques is essential to them.

Attacks by people

Chances of unpleasant encounters are slight outside the poor areas of big cities or in areas where there is known to be unrest, and it is difficult to give advice on what to do if attacked both on account of the rarity of the situation and the impossibility of anticipating the circumstances. It is prudent to hand over to a robber what he demands rather than risk a fight (your insurance should enable you to recoup your loss), but if the assailant seems incompetent or puny it could be worth attacking him. Once fighting breaks out, however, a situation becomes far more difficult to control. Robbery with violence is rare except in some unruly cities where the dangers are well known, and theft is likely to take place only in your absence. Motiveless crime is not common away from our society.

Girls are vulnerable, alone or in twos and threes, and should think twice before venturing out in small groups; adventurous souls will always go their own way, however, but should not put themselves in a position where they will be in obvious danger of being molested or where they cannot quickly summon help.

If theft is suffered, it should be reported to the police as soon as possible and in any case within 24 hours; ask for a copy of your statement, which will be required by your insurer.

Attacks by animals

The risk from rabid dogs has been mentioned. Jackals and other members of the dog family together with squirrels, bush-babies, monkeys and even bats carry rabies.

If someone is bitten by a snake, it should if possible be killed to provide positive identification and the victim should be vaccinated with the correct serum within an hour; most doctors, police stations and first aid posts in snake areas keep a serum bank but if you plan to do a lot of walking in bush or undergrowth a universal snake-bite kit should be carried and more than one person instructed in its use. With or without treatment most healthy people soon make a complete recovery, and it is important to impress this on a victim.

If a large animal seems likely to attack, move off as fast as you can; if this is not feasible, remember that animals fear fire more than noise; switch on the headlights, light a fire (set fire to the grass in a dire emergency), fire a flashgun or a flare. Do not regret your lack of a gun, which would almost certainly be useless except if it were a heavy weapon in experienced hands. Winging an animal with a low-powered weapon is cruel, illegal, pointless and liable to enrage it.

National emergencies

Foreigners who stumble into a local or national war situation will not normally be attacked or involved unless they are in some way identified with the opposite side. The have-nots may see a vehicle as a symbol of the haves, and it would be rash to attempt to drive through a demonstrating crowd or procession; sympathy with the cause would be of no help to a vehicle party marooned in a hostile gathering.

In the event of a national emergency, the best course—if it is not possible to get out in time without taking risks—is to report to your nearest embassy or consulate and follow their advice.

Weapons

An overland group should not carry firearms. Firearms cannot be carried freely in most countries and a gun will probably be sealed at the border to prevent its use. In the unlikely event of attack by armed bandits, it would be foolish to start a gun battle against their advantages of surprise, skill, and greater ruthlessness.

Marine flares, which can be carried without restriction, could double as a weapon to discourage two-legged or four-legged aggressors.

Firefighting

Petrol fires are the greatest danger. Direct an extinguisher towards the base of the flames and send other people to collect sand and soil to throw on the fire; big shovelfuls of mud or damp earth will usually smother a fire which has not reached alarming proportions. If flames approach the fuel tank or if the fire gets out of control, move right away to prevent injury by explosion. In those circumstances the fire must do its work and an insurance claim will have to be made, which is better than loss of life.

Electrical short circuits can start a smouldering fire, and the first thing to do when you smell burning is to switch everything off and remove—if necessary rip off—a battery connection. Cables should not be touched immediately as they may be red hot.

Arrest

If arrested and held, your primary and immediate objective should be to get word of your plight to your nearest embassy or consulate. The police in most countries should notify your consul but cannot always be relied on to do so. A member of the party still at liberty should contact the consul; most embassies have an officer on duty round the clock to deal with genuine emergencies.

Whatever your opinion, never give the impression that you believe the police to be behaving unreasonably; remain calm and polite, answering reasonable questions. Do not make statements which could be used against you and never sign a document unless you understand fully the implications of doing so. Insist on legal or consular advice beforehand, in any case, and on a full and trustworthy translation if the document is in an unfamiliar language.

Argument is not to be recommended, regardless of the rights and wrongs of the case, and if you find yourself in an unsatisfactory situation you should attempt to deal with an officer of higher rank.

Recording the Journey

KEEPING A DIARY

All travellers should keep a log or diary. Years later it will bring back memories which otherwise would have been lost for ever. Unless you are a compulsive diary writer it is best to settle for a few sentences every evening, outlining the day's most interesting events. The task should never be left for the next day. A diarist, in recording the striking and unusual, may ignore commonplace and characteristic features. A balanced record should contain impressions of ordinary people and their way of life. If the diarist is an artist, the record can be supplemented by or made up of sketches and drawings.

PHOTOGRAPHY

This is the easiest way of recording a journey and may be the primary motive for making it. Choice of photographic equipment varies with ability, taste and wealth, but the best equipment for the keen amateur (and even the professional travel photographer) is probably a good-quality, single lens reflex 35mm camera, preferably with through-the-lens metering and several lenses of different focal lengths. Thirty-five millimetre colour transparencies are generally acceptable for book and magazine reproduction, and for those who have their hobby or a visual record in mind, rather than commerce, will find this an economical format, with up to thirty-six exposures per film. Professionals often favour larger formats such as 6cm ($2\frac{1}{4}$in) square as the larger transparencies are preferred for blockmaking, but a large camera and an assortment of equipment is bulky and accident-prone.

When choosing a camera to take on an overland trip, it is better to look for reliability and toughness rather than complicated optical gimmicks. One of the main differences between the cheaper and more expensive single lens reflex models is the quality of construction; there is usually little to choose between them in picture-taking ability. If you cannot afford an expensive camera, consider either a secondhand high-quality model and have it thoroughly overhauled, or a simple non-reflex model which is not so likely to go wrong anyway.

It is an advantage to have two camera bodies if using a reflex system with detachable lenses in case one gives trouble, and also to allow the parallel use of colour and black and white or fast and slow film.

It is a good idea to carry equipment in a small case or holdall filled with foam plastic into which holes have been cut to suit individual items. This insulates against vibration, heat and dust and greatly reduces the risk of camera trouble.

All cameras are worth fitting with an ultra-violet filter which can be kept permanently in place, not so much to prevent mauve casts caused by excessive ultra-violet radiation in hot countries but more to protect the delicate and expensive lens from dust and accidental damage. The filter is much cheaper to replace than the lens, which should be cleaned regularly with a blower-brush and lens tissues (as should all equipment).

A medium telephoto lens to supplement the standard 50mm lens is a useful start to a collection of equipment; focal lengths of 135mm and 200mm are recommended for taking pictures of human interest which, as every newspaper picture editor knows, is what people like to see. A wide-angle lens is best for photographing buildings and street scenes but if it is not held level all the buildings will appear to be leaning backwards. It is usually a mistake to use a wide-angle lens for views even if it is tempting to record a wide panorama, as it pushes the scenery into insignificance and details practically disappear;

ideally, something of interest is needed in the foreground. A telephoto lens compresses distances in a way which is close to the mind's interpretation of a scene, and can be used to blur out a distracting background when taking portraits and similar shots.

The keen photographer will find a longer telephoto lens (perhaps a 300mm) extremely useful; it takes good 'mug shots' and its magnification lends it well to photographing game on a trans-African trip.

Long lenses are best supported when in action, but not on part of a vehicle when the engine is running; a bag or sock filled with rice, dried peas or dust-free sand makes an ideal rest. A tripod, while effective, usually takes too long to set up.

Two-times converters which screw on to a lens and double its focal length are not usually used by professional photographers because they rarely give sufficiently sharp results. If you are concerned about sharpness or hope to use your pictures commercially, it is wise to invest in extra lenses. One option not often considered is the pre-set telephoto lens, generally a lot cheaper than the automatic lens and every bit as good optically. It is usually more compact and does not take much longer to use, but is safest with through-the-lens metering.

Photographic gear should be fully insured, and cover should apply in all countries to be visited. Ordinary baggage insurance is generally inadequate for expensive equipment.

Restrict picture-taking where possible to periods when the sun is not vertically overhead. Tropical sun between the hours of 11.00 and 15.00 is usually so bright that the contrast range between sunlight and shadow is too great for most films to reproduce. In such situations, exposure must be correct for either sunlight or shadow. When photographing dark-skinned people, unless they are in the shade (where the contrast is reduced) it is best to expose for the shadows in their faces by opening the lens up a couple of stops more than the norm for such bright conditions. The slowest colour films are by far the best in situations with strong contrasts.

A meter is essential if accuracy is to be obtained in this sort of situation.

Black and white photography is less sensitive to exposure errors, particularly as much can be done to counteract mistakes at the printing stage, but it is not possible to get a crisp print from a bad negative. Black and white film is relatively cheap, and it is a safeguard against failure if several shots of a subject are taken at different angles and exposures. A good medium-speed film of about 125ASA is ideal for travel photography and can be rated at double the speed or more in poor light conditions; always note on the packet the speed of exposure if different from the recommended speed. To cope with the high contrast found in hot sunny climates, it is advisable to avoid up-rating films for use in bright sunlight as the extra development needed tends to increase the negative contrast even more and makes printing difficult.

Movies

Super-Eight is probably the most versatile format for an attractive personal record of a journey, but if you hope to sell your work it is essential to go for 16mm gauge, preferably on professional colour stock such as Ektachrome Commercial or Eastmancolor Negative at 24 or 25 frames per second depending on your market. You immediately run into extremely high costs; 16mm cameras are expensive enough, but even worse is the great expense of a sufficient footage of film. Potential commercial film makers should read Brian Branston's *A Film Maker's Guide* which warns of the pitfalls as well as giving a good idea of the possible markets and the considerable rewards to be made if you are successful. Generally, professional movie-making is not possible except for the talented and sponsored or the talented and wealthy.

Buying and storing film

Whether you take stills or movies, be sure to carry ample quantities of film. Colour film is often impossible to buy and in any case always expensive in remote areas, and you should not count on stocking up en route. Few places sell film as cheaply as the discount photographic stores in Britain and many will give a better-than-advertised discount if a large quantity is bought. Therefore, it is worth shopping for film for all members of the party simultaneously. Americans might with advantage buy film before leaving the US, and Panama, Singapore and Hong Kong offer cheap film. Buying duty-free on the cross-Channel ferries from the UK is more expensive than buying at a discount at home.

Spare film is almost as negotiable as money in many areas, although transactions may be illegal. It could be sold to other travellers, who will be taking it out of the country where the transaction took place and will not therefore be interfering with a local economy.

Black and white film is hardy and will usually give good results even after the expiry date has passed. Colour transparency film needs more care in order to prevent shifts in colour balance and loss of brightness. Heat is less hazardous than excessive humidity, but great heat from direct sunlight or the engine of the vehicle can ruin it. In hot, dry countries it is usually sufficient to pack film in a cool part of the vehicle, or with clothes. In humid areas or moist tropical rain-forest, all films and photo equipment should be kept in airtight metal containers with silica gel crystals to absorb moisture.

Do not keep film in a refrigerator; unless the packing is absolutely airtight the high humidity will spoil it. If a cold film is loaded straight away, condensation will form which could ruin the camera as well as the film.

Restrictions on photography

Some Moslems object to the photography of people because the Koran, their holy book, prohibits the representation of human beings, and unsophisticated and older people might show strong resentment at being photographed. Be circumspect when photographing in Moslem countries, therefore, and if a person indicates that a picture should not be taken the camera should be put away immediately. Pilgrims and worshippers in or near mosques and other holy places generally offer the greatest resistance so be particularly discreet in such centres as Qum and Mashad in Iran.

Be extremely careful about photographing women if you are

a man as your motives may be misunderstood, particularly so if you try taking pictures of women bathing in rivers in India where westerners have a reputation based on a heightened impression of our supposedly 'permissive society'. Women, on the other hand, can often photograph women without meeting objections. Tact is needed when photographing people anywhere, but most are flattered to be photographed if convinced that your motives are friendly and harmless.

Primitive societies are said to be afraid of cameras, but resistance is rare outside Moslem countries. The picturesque Masai people in Africa have been photographed so frequently that they often demand a large tip before they allow a picture to be taken.

Some countries have strict laws banning photography in certain areas, for example within 10km of a border. It is common for photography of what are deemed 'strategic' or 'military' installations to be prohibited; these include obvious things like military camps, airfields and warships but also such unlikely subjects as bridges, elderly steam locomotives, car-ferries and parliament buildings. Where official signs are displayed to indicate that photography is restricted (usually a picture of a camera with a line diagonally across it), and particularly in the Eastern Bloc, it is best to ask an official if it is safe to take a picture. If you are seen photographing, a policeman may demand your film and confiscate others you have.

In Mali, you can be fined and your films confiscated if you are caught photographing anything anywhere. A special permit for photography is required, available only from the tourist office in the capital, Bamako.

Wherever you are, photography of people in distressing situations should be carried out with utmost discretion and sympathy.

TAPE RECORDERS

A tape or cassette recorder is useful as a source of music while travelling and may be used to enrich a written record of a journey, or a slide or film show back at home. Recording people met on the way and playing back their voices generally causes hilarity and establishes your popularity.

Anyone with hopes of using tape recordings commercially should use a professional's machine which operates at 7in/sec.

Dust and heat are the greatest enemies of a tape recorder and it is advisable to carry it in a stout leather or metal case, preferably lined with foam plastic. Cassette players are generally best built into the dashboard of the vehicle. Cassettes, cartridges and reels of tape should, like film, be kept as cool and free from dust as possible.

Checklists: Equipment and Information

Requirements will vary from journey to journey and person to person but may be checked against these basic lists. Items considered generally essential are marked with an asterisk.

APPENDIX 1

Personal equipment
*Passport with visas
*International vaccination certificates
*International driving licence
*Personal insurance
*Spare passport photos (up to a dozen)
*Travellers' cheques and foreign currency
 International Student Card
 Sunglasses
 Camera and film
 Notebook, sketchbook, ballpoint pens, airmail envelopes
*Mug, plate, cutlery
*Torch with spare battery and bulb
 Needle and thread
 Paperback book(s)
*Sleeping bag with inner and/or blanket
*Foam plastic mattress, airbed with pump and puncture outfit, *or* light camp bed
 Mosquito net (Africa, South America, Far East)
 Detergent
*Cool clothing (cotton/terylene type rather than nylon)

*Anorak, parka or thick sweater
Set of 'best' clothes
*Footwear (one pair sandals, one pair walking)
Swimwear
*Toilet kit (with good supply of consumables)
Anti-malaria tablets (start course *before* arrival in danger zone)
Suntan lotion, lip cream, talc, insect repellent lotion and medicaments for personal health problems (hay fever, frequent headaches, etc)
Sun hat
Spare spectacles or contact lenses (plus copy of prescription)
Nail scissors
Drinking flask
Travel sickness pills

Communal equipment
*Lamp (preferably battery-operated fluorescent with spare tube)
*Tent(s)
*Cooking equipment
*Nest of saucepans or billies
*Means of water storage
*Medical kit (comprehensive)
*First aid kit (small—keep on dashboard)
*Fire extinguisher(s)
*Toilet paper
*Paper towels/tissues
Kettle
Frying pan
Pressure cooker
Refrigerator (too space-consuming if party is large)
*Storage containers
Clothes line and pegs
Insecticide (pyrethrum-based aerosol)
*Potassium permanganate crystals for sterilising fruit and vegetables
*Strong-box
Plastic washing-up bowl
Washing-up liquid and cloths
Egg container
*Can/bottle opener, corkscrew

APPENDIX 2

Vehicle documents
*Carnet de passage (east of Turkey, south of Morocco, South and Central America, many Eastern European countries)
 International certificate for motor vehicles (not always essential)
*Insurance certificate or green card
*National documents (UK: registration book, insurance certificate, roadworthiness certificate)
 Driver's certificate, journey control document and driving hours log book (vehicles with ten or more seats for travel in EEC countries)

Vehicle equipment
*Sticker to denote nationality of vehicle registration
*Reflective red warning triangles (two)
 Air horn
*Oil pressure gauge (plus oil temperature gauge for air-cooled engines)
*Water temperature gauge
 Vacuum gauge, ammeter, battery condition meter
 Engine hour meter
*Means of storing equipment
 Long-range fuel tank(s)
 Water tank(s)
 Guards for sump, track rod, headlights, axles, windscreen
 Gauze screens for windows and ventilators
 Sand tracks, chains, ladders, sand mats or other means of debogging
 Winch, hoist, or block and tackle
 Trenching tool
 Tropical roof or other heat insulation
 Soundproofing material
 Radial tyres

Chassis strengthening modifications
Heavy-duty axles/suspension
Anti-theft precautions—all external fittings
Dustproofing
Wind (dust) deflector—rear-mounted
*Spare wheel(s) and/or tyre(s)
*Full workshop manual, owner's handbook, list of agents and dealers
*Toolbox (metal) and kit as follows:
*   Open-ended spanners, complete set
*   Socket spanners, complete set with extension, universal joint, tommy bar, ratchet handle
    Ring or ring/open spanners
*   10in adjustable spanner
    3in adjustable spanner
*   Self-gripping wrench
    5in pipe wrench
*   Pliers, one long-nosed, one universal
*   Screwdrivers, various including crosshead
    Hammers, small engineer's and 2lb club
*   Wheelbrace ⎫
*   Sparking plug spanner ⎬ socket set may provide
*   Epoxy resin adhesive
    Cold chisel
    Soldering equipment
*   Radiator sealant
*   Miniature spanners, feeler gauge, fuses, insulating tape, wire, split pins
*   Nuts, bolts, washers, assorted
*   Self-tapping screws, assorted
*   Jack(s), one hydraulic, one screw
    Block, wood or metal, to support jack
    Foot pump or engine-driven airline
    Puncture outfit, tyre levers (3), spare inner tube(s)
    High pressure lever grease gun
*   Tow rope
    Hose for bleeding hydraulic systems (preferably with air exclusion valve)
    Hose for siphoning petrol (preferably clear plastic)

General spares: items already listed (eg spare inner tubes) are not repeated

Filter elements (oil, fuel, air)
Cylinder head gasket or decoke set
Valve springs, cotters, spare valve(s)
Gasket set for lower engine
Oil seals
Timing chain or belt
Engine-mounting bushes
*Spare keys
Emergency windscreen
Sealing compound
Contact adhesive
Binding wire
Sponge, handbrush

Petrol engine spares
*Ignition HT cable
*Condenser
*Points (contact breaker)
*Sparking plug(s)
*Fuel pump (or repair kit)
Ignition coil
Distributor cap and leads
Rotor arm
Carburettor overhaul kit
Length of fuel pipe
Throttle cable
Fuel pump sediment chamber (if glass)

Cooling system
*All hoses, complete set
*Fan belts (2)
Water pump, complete
Radiator cap

Transmission
*Clutch master cylinder overhaul kit
*Clutch slave cylinder overhaul kit
*Clutch cable
Clutch driving plate
Gearbox output oil seals
Half shafts (axle shafts)
Differential pinion
Seals for diff and axle
Prop shaft bearings
Rubber drive-shaft components

Brakes
*Master cylinder overhaul kit
*Wheel cylinder overhaul kits
*Servo unit overhaul kit
Flexible brake hose(s)
Length of metal brake pipe
Set brake linings/pads
Brake cable(s)

Suspension
*U-bolts and nuts
*Shock absorber bushes
Shackle plates, bolts and nuts
Spring leaves or complete spring or torsion bar (as appropriate)
Shock absorber(s), complete

Diesel engine spares
*Fuel transfer pump or overhaul kit
*Heater (glow plug)
Heater circuit resistance
Injector(s)
High pressure fuel lines and unions
Injection pump, complete
Injection pump drive shaft

Fuel pump sediment chamber (if glass)
Length of fuel pipe (low pressure)
Throttle cable

Electrical system
*Fuses
*Bulbs (extra head and rear)
*Cable, connectors
*Diode set (for alternator system only)
Generator brushes
Starter motor brushes
Starter motor relay solenoid
Voltage control box, complete
Jump leads
Second battery

Wheels and hubs
*Valve cores and caps
Wheel bearing set(s)
Wheel oil seals
Wheel nut and stud
Extra spare wheel

Steering
Track rod ends
Steering joint rubber dust cover(s)
Steering damper

Consumable materials
*Engine oil (1 complete change)
*Transmission oil
*Brake and clutch fluid (1 quart)
Grease
Epoxy and/or fibreglass kit
Ether aerosol
Electrical waterproofing aerosol
Light lubricating oil

APPENDIX 3

(Medical Kit)

Medicines listed are easily obtained and known to be effective; the list is not exhaustive, however, and a doctor or pharmacist will be able to suggest substitutes.

Warning: preparations containing steroids can be dangerous and must not be used without proper medical supervision.

General
Water-sterilising tablets and/or stabilised bleach powder
Salt tablets
Multivitamin tablets (to supplement canned-food diets)

External
Cetavlon, Savlon, Dettol ointments (cleaning wounds, burns)
Canestan (clotrimazole), magenta and benzoic acid compound ointment (fungicide for athlete's foot and similar)
Zinc undecenoate powder (preventive: athlete's foot and similar)
Optrex (eye discomfort)
Chloramphenicol eye drops BPC, sulphacetamide eye drops BPC (conjunctivitis)
Calamine lotion (skin sedative)

Digestive system
Milk of Magnesia (mild indigestion, nausea, constipation)
Aludrox (indigestion, heartburn)
Mil-par, Senokot, Dulcolan (constipation)
Kaolin compound (Lomotil), codeine phosphate tablets (diarrhoea)

Drugs
Treatment must not be given if patient has suffered side effects

from former treatment; note particularly aspirin and penicillin in this context.

Aspirin, codeine, paracetamol (headaches, minor pain, influenza)
DF118 (dihydrocodeine tartrate) (severe pain)
Benylin, Phensedyl, Cosylan (cough mixtures and expectorants)
Strepsils (minor infections of mouth and throat)
Anthisan, Benodryl, Phenergan (antihistamine preparations for treatment of allergies such as skin rashes, hay fever)

Antibiotics
Penicillin V (phenoxymethylpenicillin) (sepsis)
Oxytetracycline (to control development of fever; suitable for those allergic to penicillin)
Penbritin (ampicillin) (severe respiratory, urinary or gastrointestinal conditions; not suitable for those allergic to penicillin)

Treatment of wounds
Cotton wool, sterile gauze, non-stick dry dressing
Adhesive plasters, assorted
Surgical adhesive plaster, assorted widths
Bandages, roll, crepe, triangular, assorted
Adhesive (butterfly) sutures

Other equipment
Scissors, fine and blunt-ended
Tweezers, fine
Safety pins, assorted
Inflatable splints
Clinical thermometer
First aid manual (St John Ambulance Brigade or similar)

APPENDIX 4

Documents
Department of the Environment, 2 Marsham Street, London SW1P 3EB (01-212 3434)

Main Passport Office, Petty France, London SW1 (01-222 8010)

(Also AA and RAC—addresses under *Travel information*)

Medical
Hospital For Tropical Diseases, St Pancras Way, London NW1 (01-387 4411)

Medical Department, British Airways Terminal, Victoria, London (01-834 2323)

West London Vaccination Centre, 53 Great Cumberland Place, London W1 (01-262 6456)

Travel information
Automobile Association, Fanum House, Basing View, Basingstoke, Hampshire (Basingstoke 20123)

Consular Department, Foreign and Commonwealth Office, Clive House, Petty France, London SW1H 9HD (01-930 2323)

Royal Automobile Club, 83-5 Pall Mall, London SW1Y 5HZ (01-930 4343)

Shell International Petroleum, Shell Centre, London SE1 (01-934 1234)

APPENDIX 5

Phrasebooks of principal eastern and African languages are not readily obtainable but the overlander may need at least the words given below in a phonetic form. The Iranian petrol pump (*Plate 4*) illustrates Persian and Arabic numerals.

		Swahili		*Arabic*
hello	hu jambo	*hoo-jarmbo*		*er-hlaan-waa-ser-hlaan*
goodbye	kwa heri	*kwahairy*		*maaserlayma*
please	tafadhali	*tafardali*		*m'n-f'd-l'k*
thank you	ahsante	*are-sunntey*		*shukren*
yes	naam	*narm*		*nam*
no	siyo	*see-yoh*		*ley*
how much?	kiasi gani?	*kee-arsey gani*		*kem*
petrol	petrol	*petrolli*		*betrole*
diesel	diesel	*dieselli*		*gaz*
water	maji	*marjey*		*mey*
food	chakula	*chuckoola*		*ekerl*
bread	mkate	*umcartey*		*hobbs*
enough	baasi	*barssi*		*beyhi*
1	moja	*mohjah*		*waherd*
2	mbili	*umbeelee*		*neen*
3	tatu	*tartoo*		*tlaita*
4	nne	*n'nay*		*arba*
5	tano	*tarno*		*hummsa*
6	sita	*seeta*		*seeta*
7	saba	*sarba*		*saba*
8	nane	*narnay*		*tmenyer*
9	tisa	*teesa*		*teesa*
10	kumi	*koomi*		*ashra*
11	kumi na moja	*koomi na mohjah*		*ehada-ashar*
12	kumi na mbili	*koomi na umbeeli*		*ithne-ashar*
13	kumi na tatu	*koomi na tartoo*		*telaitete-ashar*
14	kumi na nne	*koomi na n'nay*		*erba'ete-ashar*
15	kumi na tano	*koomi na tarno*		*hummsete-ashar*
20	ishirini	*ishereenee*		*ashreen*
50	hamsini	*hamseenee*		*humseen*
100	mia	*mee-ar*		*mee-ah*
1,000	elfu	*elfoo*		*elf*
½	nusu	*nusoo*		*nusf*

	Turkish		Persian	
hello	meraba	meraba	salám alékom	se-larm allaykom
goodbye	allah ismarladik	uller-ushmarlad'k	khodá háfez	horda harfez
please	lütfen	leutfen	lotfan	lotfan
thank you	teşekkür ederim	tesherkeur-ederim	merci/tasakkor	mairsee/tush-akkor
yes	evet	evet	balé	ba-lay
no	hayir	hyoh	na	nar
how much?	ne kadar?	n'kadar	chand?	chund
petrol	benzin	ben-zin	benzin	bendsin
diesel	mazot/diesel	muzzoht/di-zell	dizel	di-zell
water	su	soo	áb	ob
food	gida	girder	ghaza	khaza
bread	ekmek	ekmek	nán	nom
enough	tamam	tumm-arm	kafi	khafi
1	bir	beer	yek	yek
2	iki	icki	dô	daw
3	üc	ertch	se	say
4	dört	dirt	chahar	ch-har
5	beş	besh	panj	punch
6	alti	ulter	shesh	shish
7	yedi	yaidee	haft	huffed
8	sekiz	seckers	hasht	hushed
9	dokuz	dockers	noh	naw
10	on	ong	dah	dar
11	on bir	ong beer	yazdah	yuz-dar
12	on iki	ong icki	davazdah	de-vuzzdar
13	on üç	ong ertch	sizdah	seez-dar
14	on dört	ong dirt	cháhrdah	chore-dar
15	on beş	ong besh	pánzdah	paanch-dar
20	yirmi	yirmee	bist	beest
50	elli	eller	panjah	punn-jaw
100	yüz	yirz	sad	sudd
1,000	bin	bin	hazar	huz-zaw
½	yarim	yarrim	nim	neem

Bibliography

Adam, Lt-Colonel James M., *A Traveller's Guide to Health* (Royal Geographical Society, 1966; Sphere, 1968)
Alderson, Frederick, *The New Grand Tour* (David & Charles, 1971)
Baker, Michael H. C., *Journey to Katmandu* (David & Charles, 1974)
Byron, Robert, *The Road to Oxiana* (Jonathan Cape, repr, 1937)
Coleman, John, *Coleman's Drive: From Buenos Aires to New York in a Vintage Baby Austin* (Faber & Faber, 1962)
Galton, Sir F., *The Art of Travel* (David & Charles, repr, 1971)
Grenville, G. M., *Cruising the Sahara* (David & Charles, 1974)
Hillaby, John, *Journey to the Jade Sea* (Constable & Co, 1964)
——, *Journey Through Europe* (Constable & Co, 1972)
Jenkins, David, *Student Guide to Asia* (Australian Union of Students, 1974)
Murphy, Dervla, *Full Tilt: Ireland to India with a Bicycle* (John Murray/Pan, 1965)
Newby, Eric, *A Short Walk in the Hindu Kush* (Hodder & Stoughton, 1972)
——, *Slowly Down the Ganges* (Hodder & Stoughton, 1966)
Nicholson, T. R., *The Wild Roads: The Story of Transcontinental Motoring* (Jarrolds, 1969)
Shultz, Mick, *Traveler's Guide to West Africa* (Multivers, Copenhagen, 1973)
——, *Asia for the Hitch-Hiker* (Multivers, Copenhagen, 1973)
Slessor, Tim, *First Overland: The Story of the Oxford and Cambridge Far Eastern Expedition* (Harrap, 1957)
Smith, Anthony, *Blind White Fish in Persia* (George Allen & Unwin, 1953)
——, *High Street Africa* (George Allen & Unwin, 1960)
Stephens, Sir R., *The Land of the Great Sophy* (Methuen, 1963)

Toy, Barbara, *The Highway of the Three Kings, The Way of The Chariots, In Search of Sheba, A Fool on Wheels, Columbus Was Right* (John Murray, various dates)
Tschiffley, A. F., *Southern Cross to Pole Star* (later *Tschiffley's Ride*) (Heinemann, 1933)
Walsh, Ken, *Hitch-Hiker's Guide to Europe* (Pan, 1974)

MAPS AND GUIDES

A Traveller's Guide to Africa (African Buyer & Trader (Publications), London, 1974)
Blue Guides, The: *The Middle East* (Hachette, Paris, various dates)
Dupree, Nancy Hatch, *An Historical Guide to Afghanistan* (Afghan Tourist Organisation, Kabul, 1971)
Fodor's Guides: *Islamic Asia*; *Tunisia*; *Morocco*; *Turkey*; *South America* (Hodder & Stoughton, various dates)
Lascelles, Roger, *Asia Overland* map (Lascelles, London, 1973)
Michelin Maps: West Africa (153); North East Africa (154); Southern Africa (155); Morocco (169); Northern Algeria (172); Ivory Coast (175); also Europe
Nagel's Guides: *Thailand*; *Algeria*; *Brazil*; *Peru*; *Lebanon*; *Egypt*; *China*; *USSR*; *Iran*; *Morocco*; *Turkey* (Nagel, Geneva, various dates)

Index

AA, 13, 16, 39, *Appendix* 4
Accessories, for vehicles, 62
Accidents, 16, 107, 127
Accounting, 37
Air beds, 55
Air horns, 64
altitude, driving at high, 94
animals, 78, 115, 129
Arabic, *Appendix* 5
Arrest, 131
Attacks, by people or animals, 115
Austin; 4x4 lorry, 26; Gipsy 26;
  Champ, 26
Automatic transmission, 25
Axles, reinforced, 70

Bazaars, 125
Beach buggies, 28
Bedding, 54
Bedford; CF, 28; RL, 26;
  Utilabrake, 28
Bicycles, 21
Bilharzia, 85, 123
Black markets, 35
Boats, travel by, 20
Bodges, 105-7
Border crossings, 111
Brake; fade, 93; failure, 93, 106
Breakdowns, 21, 104, 128
British Leyland; J4 & 250JU vans,
  28; *see* Land-Rover, Mini, Mini-
  Moke, Range-Rover
Buses, travel by, 21

Cadence braking, 95
Cameras, 132
Camp bed, 55
Camping, 113ff
Camping carnet, 40
Canned food, 15, 56, 74
Caravan conversions, 23, 27, 28,
  29
Caravette, VW, 27
Carnet de passage, 13, 16, 40
Cars, 21, 28
Cash, 34
Chains, tyre, 64, 88
Champ, Austin, 26
Citroën 2CV, 29
Climatic conditions, 13
Clothes, 55, 110
Clutch slip, 107
Commer, 28
Commercial overland trips, 19
Companions, 18
Containers, 74
Cookers; gas, 48; paraffin, 53;
  petrol, 52; pressure, 53
Cooking equipment, 48
Corrugated roads, 24, 81
Costs, 14ff, 37
Crocodile hoist, 65
Currency, 33ff

Debogging techniques, 88ff
Deserts, 23; *see* sand, dust,
  climatic conditions

153

Dexion, 75
Diaries, 132
Diesel engines, 21
Documents, 37ff
Drivers and driving, 76ff
Driving cross-country, 90
Driving licence, 14; international, 17, 39
Drugs, 32
Dust, 66, 71, 74, 80

Economy, fuel, 69
EEC control document, 42
Eggs, 59
Emergencies, 16, 95, 126ff
Equipment, general, 47ff
Exchange rates, 35-6

Farsi (Persian), *Appendix* 5
Fire, 130
Firearms, 130
Fire extinguisher, 27, 62, 130
First aid, 60, *Appendix* 3
Food, 53, 56ff, 116ff
Ford; Thames, 28; Transit, 28
Fording rivers, 82ff
Four-wheel drive, 21, 22ff, 73, 86, 91ff
Free-wheeling hubs, 69
Freeze-dried food, 56
Frontier crossings, 111
Fruit, 117, 124
Fuel; availability, 96; consumption, 18, 24-5; economy, 69; prices, 12, 15, 18, 22; tanks, long range, 63

Gaiters for tyres, 104
Garages, 99
Gas Cookers, 48
Gipsy, Austin, 26
Green card, 16
Ground clearance, 22, 26, 28
Guards; sump, 64; windscreen, 64; chaff, 64
Guide books, 13

Haflinger, 25
Haggling, 125

Hashish, *see* drugs
Hazards driving, 77
Highwayman, Commer, 28
Hitch-hiking, 20
Horns, hooters, 64
Housekeeping equipment, 59
Humber 4x4 lorry, 26

Iceboxes, 53
Illness, 16, 20
Information, sources of, 12
Insects, 116
Instruments, 62
Insulation, 66
Insurance, 14ff, 34, 40, 44ff, 76, 129, 131, 134
International certificate for motor vehicles, *Appendix* 2
International driving license, 17, 39
Islamic countries, 110ff

Jeep, 26
Jerrycans, 55, 63

Kitty, 37, 118
Kombi, VW, 27

Land-Cruiser, Toyota, 25
Land-Rover, 23ff, 62, 65, 69-75
Languages, 97, *Appendix* 5
License, driving, 17, 33, 39

License disc, tax, 40
Link Travel, 19
Loading, 74

Mail, 45ff
Maintenance, 98
Malaria, 60, 116
Maps, 12, 96-7
Mechanical checks, 71, 98
Medical equipment, 60, *Appendix* 3
Microbus, VW, 27
Mini, British Leyland, 29
Minibuses, 21, 27
Mini Moke, British Leyland, 28
Modifications to vehicles, 62ff

Money, 33ff
Mopeds, 21
Mosquito nets, 54, 64
Mosquitoes, 47, 113, 114, 116
Motorcycles, 21, 29, 127
Motorised caravans, 28-9, 51
Mountain passes, 92
Mountainous areas, 24
Mud, 24, 65, 88, 90

Navigation, 96ff
Night driving, 77

Officials, 20, 111
Optimus stove, 52
Overdrive, 69
Overheating, 27, 63, 92, 106
Overland trips, commercial, 19
Overlanders, other, 112
Overloading, 21-2, 28, 72

Packing, 74
Pan American Highway, 11
Passengers, 31
Passports, 14, 17, 37
People, problems with, 108ff
Persian, *Appendix* 5
Petrol engines, 21
Peugot, 29
Photography, 32, 132ff
Police, 112, 114
Poste restante, 45
Pots and pans, 53
Power steering, 25
Preparations, 31ff
Pressure cooker, 53
Propane, *see* gas
Public transport, 20
Punctures, 104
Purification of water, 122

Rabies, 116, 129
RAC, 13, 16, 39, *Appendix* 4
Radios, 56
Railways, 20
Ramadan, 111
Range-Rover, 25
Refrigerators, 53
Renault, 4, 29

Repairs, 15, 10ff, 105-7
Restaurants, 109, 116
Retreads, 104
River boats, 20
Roadholding, 23, 70
Roads, 80ff
Roof; canvas, 24; tropical, 24, 66
Roofracks, 72, 75

Safety belts, 126
Sand, 65, 86, 87ff
Sandstorms, 87
Sand tracks/ladders, 65, 89
Scooters, 21, 30
Scorpions, 47, 116
Servicing, 99
Shock absorbers, 70
Skidding, 76, 80, 81, 95-6
Slippery roads, 88, 92
Sleeping bag, 47, 54
Smallpox vaccinations, 42-3
Snakes, 116, 129
Soft road surfaces, 86ff
Sound proofing, 66
Space blanket, 47, 54
Spare parts, 23, 25, 27, 28, 62,
  Appendix 2
Sponsorship, 31
Springs; breakage, 107;
  strengthening, 69
Sterilising water, 123-4
Sump guard, 64
Suspensions, 69, 98, 107
Swahili, *Appendix* 5

Tanks, water and fuel, 63
Tape recorders, 137
Telegrams, 46
Temperature gauge, 27, 62-3
Tents, 47
Thames, Ford, 28
Theft, 16, 34, 36, 45, 129
Third party insurance, 15, 44
Tools, 61-2, 74, *Appendix* 2
Toyota Land Cruiser, 25
Tracks, 11, 80ff
Trail Finders, 19
Trailers, 66, 72-3, 75, 76
Transit, Ford, 28, 71

Transporter, VW, 27
Travellers cheques, 33
Tropical Diseases, Hospital for, 43, *Appendix* 4
Tropical roof, 24, 66
Turkish, *Appendix* 5
Two-wheel drive, 26, 65, 86
Tyres, 69, 70, 104

U bolts, 98
Unimog, Mercedes, 25
Utilabrake, Bedford, 28

Vaccinations, 42ff
Vaccination certificates, 39
Vacuum flasks, 53
Vacuum gauge, 69
Valuables, 55
Vans, 27, 28-9
Vapour lock, 94
Vegetables, 117, 124
Vehicle, choice of, 21ff
Visas, 14, 38-9
Volkswagen, 27-8, 62, 71, 84; Kombi, 27; Microbus, 27; Transporter, 27; VW 181, 28

Walking, 19, 128
Warning triangles, 62, 128
Washboard roads, *see* corrugated roads
Water; bags, 54; drinking, 63; 118ff; fording, 82ff; purification, 122-4; tanks, 63
Weapons, 130
Weather, 13
Wheelbase, choice of, 24
Wild animals, 78-9, 115-6, 129
Winches, 65, 85, 89
Windscreen; emergency, 64, 107; guards, 64
Work permits etc, 31
Writing, 32, 132

Yellow fever vaccination, 42-3
Yellow headlights, 72

CARAWAGON COMFORT
for the hardened traveller

CARAWAGON INTERNATIONAL LTD
THAMES STREET SUNBURY ENGLAND TEL 85205

BY APPOINTMENT TO
HER MAJESTY THE QUEEN
MANUFACTURERS OF SPECIALISED TRAILERS
CARAWAGON INTERNATIONAL LIMITED
SUNBURY ON THAMES

TRAIL FINDERS
The Overland Information Centre

The only organisation of its kind
in the world specialising in
*Expedition travel to India,
Africa and through Latin America
*Worldwide economy flights
*Advice for the independent
traveller

Write or call for our free colour
newspaper

**Trail Finders Ltd
48 (N) Earls Court Road
London W8 6EJ England
Telephone (01) 937 9631**

DON'T MONKEY AROUND
WITH YOUR INSURANCE COVER

MAKE SURE YOU HAVE ADEQUATE COVER FOR:

Overseas Motor Insurance
Medical Expenses
Personal Accident
Cancellation & Curtailment
Baggage

FOR EXPERT ADVICE AND QUOTATION CONTACT:

Charles Angus & Co
193 Victoria Street
London SW1
Tel. 01-828 7595/6

SLUGOCKI, NORMAN & CO LTD
Insurance Brokers

48 Earls Court Road, London W8 6EJ
Telephone (01) 937 6981 Telex 919670

INSURANCE FOR OVERLAND TRAVELLERS

OVERSEAS MOTOR

Accidental damage Fire and Theft
Facilities to protect your vehicle or motorcycle against Accidental Damage, Fire or Theft, normally on a worldwide basis.

Third Part Liability
Facilities to protect your liability for damage or injury caused to other people or their property. Subject to geographical limits or legislation but we can arrange cover for a wider area than is normally available.

Carnet Indemnity
An indemnity can be arranged to protect your liability in the event of duty becoming payable or simply to enable carnet documents to be issued without a lump sum being frozen in this country.

Marine Transit
A policy can be arranged against those risks not covered by a motor policy whilst a vehicle is being shipped.

PERSONAL
Medical expenses
Probably the most important risk. Cover is available for expedition travellers medical expenses, including in an emergency, repatriation costs to the United Kingdom.

Personal accident
As with medical expenses a policy specifically designed for overland expedition travel.

Cancellation and curtailment
To protect payments made to an operator if you are unable to commence the trip or a proportion of the cost if you are forced to curtail the trip.

Life Assurance
A necessity at home and even more so when on an overland trip.

Overland Expeditions can be hazardous and insurance to cover the various risks is difficult to arrange. We have facilities with leading British and Continental companies. Lloyds and offices as far afield as Poland and Afghanistan. We shall be pleased to assist you with any problems you may have.

CAMPBELL IRVINE LTD
Insurance Brokers

48 Earls Court Road London W8 6EJ
Telephone 01 937 9903 Telex 919670

"Do you want it wrapped....

or will you take it as it is"

We specialise in unpackaged travel.

So, if you want to plan your own adventure, or cross the world with one of the many overland expedition organisers we represent, have a talk with us first.

You'll find a world of difference.

There's overland adventure on every continent. Trans Africa, Asia and South America, and safaris in Ethiopia and Kenya.

There's trekking expeditions to the Roof of the World. Annapurna and Everest Base Camp treks October 75 — March 76, 24 days from £410 fully inclusive.

And in 1976, there's the first ever expedition to Ladakh and Leh and the chance to see the famous monasteries of Little Tibet.

Keep in touch with what's happening in the world of overland travel with OVERLAND, the magazine that's packed with news, facts and information.

Give us a ring, or drop us a line, and discover the real world of travel.

Link
THE OVERLAND TRAVEL AGENCY

Link Travel
3 Bedford Road
London W.4
tel: 01-994 7668

ENCOUNTER OVERLAND

THE WORLD'S MOST ADVENTUROUS LONG RANGE EXPEDITIONS

Explore the remote regions of **AFRICA, ASIA,** and **SOUTH AMERICA.** Our specially designed vehicles enable us to take the less travelled routes. Forget about alarming fuel costs, inevitable maintenance problems, those expensive carnets and difficult to obtain road permits. Get out from underneath your landrover and fully experience new peoples and places. See **Africa, Asia** and **South America** as they should be seen — while they are still a bit different!

From 11 weeks for £445 fully inclusive. For details of expeditions and film evenings contact:

ENCOUNTER OVERLAND
280 Old Brompton Road
London S.W.5
01-370-6845

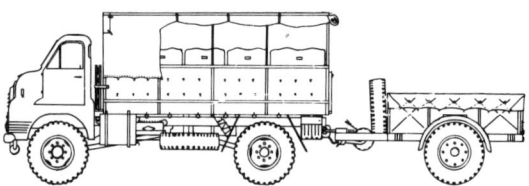

TVC'S AIR-CAMPERS

Up in One Minute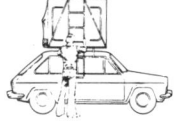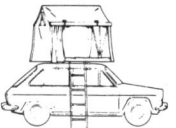

A FULLY EQUIPPED CARTOP TENT

FITS — CARS, VANS, AND LAND ROVERS

Travels as weatherproof luggage rack, converts quickly to hotel-comfortable bed large enough for two adults and a child. Complete with travel cover, mattress, and mounting rack. *Only £92 plus VAT.*

MOST INEXPENSIVE VAN CONVERSION

SAFARI TESTED

Hundreds in Use in Africa

TVC LTD
30 Berkeley House, Hay Hill
London W1. Tel (01) 499-1164

Roof Racks *Made from heavy duty box section, finished in blued silver hammer*

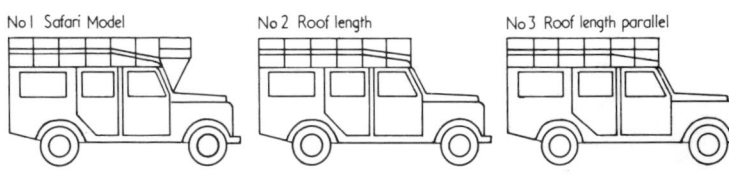

No 1 Safari Model   No 2 Roof length   No 3 Roof length parallel

Bob and Joe Williams offer Land-Rover racks from stock in our original designs using ¾sq x 14G. tube. All other racks for vans and customers own designs can be made up within three days. We also supply Jerry-cans and holders, sand ladders and anything in steel for overland travellers.

P.S. We also offer light-hearted conversation and nerve tonic to any apprehensive would-be overlanders.

WILCO ENGINEERING

GENERAL ENGINEERING & WELDING

Arch 422, Burdett Road
Bow — London — E3

Telephone 01-987-1767

'Overland' with David & Charles

Journey to Katmandu
Michael Baker

This book describes a three-month journey from England to Katmandu and home again. The route covered by 46 young people, travelling in somewhat spartan conditions in three ex RAF lorries named Faith, Hope and Charity, was through France, Italy, Yugoslavia, Bulgaria, Turkey, Iran and on into Afghanistan, India and Nepal. The return journey was a leisurely one by train and boat from Moscow through Leningrad, Helsinki, Stockholm and the Hook of Holland. The book is illustrated with drawings by the author and many photographs.

Cruising the Sahara
Gerard Morgan-Grenville

The author has lurched through Morocco on a camel, sped along in a package tour, skimmed past rolling dunes in a sand yacht and coaxed his Land-Rover back and forth across the greatest desert on earth and here for the first time the different methods of travel are compared, catalogued and costed. This book is a must for aspiring desert travellers.

LAND ROVER Safari prep

We cover all your Landrovers needs for trips anywhere – full services for any distance.

Special Preparation Jerricans and holders, sand ladders, sump guards, light guards, crash bars, winches, freewheeling hubs, flyscreens, chamois leather gaiters, heavy duty half shafts for 2 and 2A vehicles, tropical roofs, long range fuel tanks, heavy duty suspension, steering dampers, prop guards, heavy duty towing plates and hooks, lifting rings, sand and ranger tyres, Water purifying plants, suspension seats, etc.

Roof Racks We design and manufacture the finest quality roof racks made from heavy duty box section tube, Custom made if required.

* Crypton tuning, short blocks, exchange engines, diffs, radiators, gear boxes, S.P. housings, etc.

Service, maintenance, wide selection of spares for Land and Range Rovers. Overdrive units available for all models of Land Rover.

For all enquiries phone or write (enclosing s.a.e.) to Dept 'E',

Brownchurch (Components) Ltd.
Arch 420/421, Burdett Road, London E.3.   Telephone: 01–987 6640/3174.

LAND-ROVER SPARES

LONDON'S LARGEST STOCKISTS OF NEW, USED AND RECONDITIONED PARTS

SPECIALISTS in ex-military and safari equipment. Distributors of Fairy Winch Products. Overdrive units, free-wheel hubs.

LIMITED SLIP DIFFERENTIALS, exchange gearboxes, diffs., engines, jerrycans and holders, fuel tanks, sand ladders, door tops. Dunlop and Maloja dual purpose tyre stockists.

ROOF RACKS and ROOF TENTS for all models.

Land-Rovers bought, sold and exchanged

P. F. FOLEY (LAND-ROVERS)
2a Herbert Road, Tottenham, London, N.15
01-808 2256   S.A.E.   01-808 8824

DUNSFOLD
LAND-ROVER SPECIALISTS

- Vehicles — Spares
- Wide Ranging Stock
- Free Advisory Service

Tel: Dunsfold (048 649) 567
Write: Land-Rovers
       Dunsfold
       Surrey GU8 4NP

There's no substitute for the versatile Land-Rover

Around one million examples have been produced, finding worldwide employment on every exercise from famine relief and mountain rescue to frontier patrolling and glider launching. Servicing is easy and infrequent and there are some 15,000 variants. Ask your dealer for details.

Tarpaulin and Tent Mfg Co

Head Office & Main Showrooms
101/3 Brixton Hill, London, SW2.
Tel: (01)–674 0121/3

We are the experts and suppliers to most commercial and private expeditions. Tents, from the large ex-WD Marquees to lightweight 2-man nylon tents, camp beds, air beds, stoves, mosquito nets, sand ladders, jerricans (water and petrol), wire ropes and slings, towing chains, all types of ropes and tarpaulins.

We also repair tents. We are stockists of all leading branded goods, Black's Tilley, Optimus, Dudley, PTC-Europleasure, Marechal, Tillbrook, Relum, Campari, etc. Calor Gas Stockists.

Branch at 137 Clapham High Street, SW4. Tel: (01)–720 5451
Barclaycard & Access

Send 10p stamp to Head Office for CATALOGUE

YOU CAN'T TRAVEL WITHOUT MAPS

We have a unique range of stock to meet the needs of every kind of traveller and map user.

Maps for the business man, trekker, tourist, motorist, walker and cyclist.

Maps for every kind of outdoor leisure – yachting, canoeing, mountain hiking, orienteering, hunting.

Maps for the specialist – geological and thematic.

Large scale maps for town planners, developers and house buyers.

Town plans, guide books, gazetteers, atlases, globes.

Stockists for the Ordnance Survey; French Official Survey (I.G.N.); other foreign surveys; the Directorate of Overseas Surveys and Directorate of Military Survey.

Edward Stanford Limited
The International Map Centre
12-14 Long Acre
London WC2E 9LP